Your Paperless E-Book Publishing Blueprint

Your Paperless E-Book Publishing Journey 1

How to Profit from Your Info Product 3

What You Need 5

Planning Your Info Product Creation 7

Creating Your Info Product 15

Contents 25

Joining Affiliate Programs 31

Info Product Creation Tips 35

In Closing 37

Recommended Resources 38

Module 2: Info Product Business Setup Explained 39

The 3 Business Models You Can Choose From 41

What You Need 50

Writing Your Sales Letter 53

How to Create a Back-End Sale in Your Thank You Page 73

Setting Up Your Business 74

Recommended Resources 86

Module 3: Online Marketing Explained 87

The Truth about SEO 89

Preparing Your Promotion Materials 92

Endorsing to Your Mailing List..97

Leverage on Affiliate Marketing...98

Recommended Resources For Starting Your Own Affiliate Program 99

Ad Swaps...102

Low Cost Advertising that Works 104

The Closing..109

Recommended Resources..110

Your Paperless E-Book Publishing Journey

Dear Valued Reader,

Good evening and thank you for investing in your Information Product education.

You are probably convinced on how profitable the information market can be. And in cases more than one, I admit that the profitability in the information market can be, most of the time, out of my own realm of imagination.

So much so, indeed, that it's rather **fascinating.**

Also, I trust that you already know that this package has been divided into 3 instructional Modules.

Obviously, I hazard a guess you will be starting your Info Product profits education with this manual.

In a nutshell, the 3 Modules required of you to succeed in being an Infopreneur are:

    Creating a product,   -   (covered in this module)

    Setting up your business, and   -   (covered in Module #2)

    Market it!   -   (covered in Module #3)

While these steps may sound absurdly oversimplified and have been told in many versions, I'll show you how making money online with your own Info Products is done.

As the title of this manual is rather self explanatory, you will also quickly learn that this manual **itself** is a perfect example of an Info Product that sells. At first glance, to some, it may look as if I have just created an Info Product that teaches others how to create one.

But you will also discover that **I really DO practice what I teach**, having been of service to some of my faithful clients as a ghostwriter and created several Info Products and Private Label products that sells.

I've said it before, but it bears repeating: it takes **all** of the Modules (which are presented in this package) to succeed and profit in the information market.

If you have at least one weak Module or more, your business can be doomed to fail. **It is that crucial.**

Now, I strongly recommend that you start with this manual, whether you haven't written your first Info Product that sells just yet or not.

At the end of this manual, I know you WILL learn something new, even if you are a seasoned information entrepreneur.

Now, let's get started. The earlier you begin, the faster you can rake in your profits in the information market. So here's the scoop from me – how to create your own Info Product out of thin air!

To Your Paperless E-Book Publishing Success!

How to Profit from Your Info Product

Upfront Sales

This is self-explanatory. You make this type of money simply by first selling to your customers.

Back end Income

You earn this kind of income from the same customer through your links embedded within your E-Book.

If the same customer purchases something through your link or affiliate link, you earn additional income to the upfront sales from the same customer.

The income can be recurring if your link or affiliate link is a membership or service site.

Conveying Resell Rights

You can sell your same product at a higher price by giving your customer, especially a reseller, the right to resell your product.

For example, your product is priced at $97.00 then perhaps your Resell Rights price can be $397.00.

Savvy customers or resellers can afford such a price and know too well that it takes only after 4 sales to profit from the sales of your product.

(Now, you know how I turned a $57.00 product into a $550.00 product)

The subject of Resell Rights is covered in detail in the report "3 Steps to Profiting from Your Resell Rights Business".

Selling Its Source Format

This type of rights is probably the most expensive type of rights there is in Internet Marketing.

In a nutshell, you are selling your product's Private Label Rights, which is the editable Word document, to your customers, who are likely to be Internet Marketers.

Since savvy marketers are often busy individuals and some of them just don't have the knack to create their own product, you can sell your product's source format at 5 to 10 times the price, maybe more.

This is the basis of the manual, Guide to Private Label Rights, where it shows you how you can profit from selling Private Label Rights in detail.

What You Need

Word Program

You will need a Word Program to start creating your own Information Product (E-Book). If you are Microsoft user like me, you should find the Microsoft Word program readily installed within your computer's system.

PDF Converter Program

Once you have finished creating your own Information Product and proof-read it for the last time, you will need a program that can convert your Word document into PDF format.

That way, your product cannot be altered, add, removed, edited, and its contents remain intact and just the way the document was before you converted it.

You can also disable the copying function to prevent convenient content theft copying.

I am currently using the PDF converter, which is already available within [the suite](#) where I am hosting my web site at, to convert my Word documents into PDF products.

Alternatively, you can PDF converter services such as [OpenOffice](#).

Recommended Resource: This [PDF Tool Kit](#) is yours as a bonus to purchasing this package. Its retail price is $19.95, but that should help you save at least $400.00 from using Adobe's PDF converter program.

Attention:

Contrary to popular recommendations, I **DON'T** endorse using PDF995 to convert your Word documents.

This is because you will learn that the links within your document would not be clickable, rendering your product useless for back-end income from the same reader / customer.

Paint Program (optional)

While this is optional, you will probably need a Paint Program to create your Word document's cover and maybe other parts of your product where images and illustrations might be needed.

I use **Adobe Photoshop** program to create my own covers (see the first page of this E-Book for example).

The topic on creating your own cover will be covered in detail later.

Affiliate Programs You Join

You have to join at least a few quality affiliate programs so that you can recommend them to your customers in your paid Info Product in order to enable back end income.

The topic on joining affiliate programs will be covered in detail later.

Your Brain with Some Confidence to Go!

Now, this is something you CANNOT go without when it comes to creating your own Info Product for sale.

Planning Your Info Product Creation

Here are 9 important aspects to consider before starting your own Info Product creation.

1. **Demand**

Internet Marketers often associate the term "niche" with this topic, but in a nutshell, what you really want to ask yourself is, "who are my customers?"

In other words, who is looking for a demand and is willing to pay for it? And then, how many of them?

As in the case of creating your own Info Product for sale, you want to know what kind of information people are looking for, are willing to pay for it, and there are many of them.

If you have yet to research your own target market you want to cater to, I strongly recommend that you download Good Keywords software [here](#).

You will find out how you can quickly discover what people are already looking for in a very short time.

As you might already know, what you personally like or know may sometimes be of little importance (or even profits) when it comes to choosing your target market, unless what you know or do are what people are willing to pay to learn, find out, or acquire.

For example: If you are Self Help practitioner for over 10 years, then you can cash in on your Self Help wisdom by selling what you know and practice on various aspects of Self Help, such as time management, stress handling, and more, to people who are low in self esteem (many of these folks around, by the way, we're all human).

On the other hand, it would be next-to-impossible to sell what you know on how to conquer the game of Tic Tac Toe.

While many people of different countries and cultures have at least played this game once in their child hoods, no one really cares about even losing in a game of 9 boxes.

You've guessed it – no one is willing to pay for what you know, even if you know how to win the game of Tic Tac Toe for sure.

2. **Price**

While you can put it down to pricing your product according to its quality, however way you judge it, you have to take the size of the market into consideration.

It's obvious you purchased a copy of this manual so that you can cash in on your own Information Product Empire.

And assuming you want to make $10,000.00 (or even more), which way is the best? Low price, high volume? Or high price, low volume?

Little you might know, it has a lot to do with the size of your market.

Now, here's a food for thought: if your market size is extravagantly huge, you can sell your product at a low price, but go for volume and still achieve your $10,000.00 goal (if that IS your goal).

This aspect is important, because if your market size is small, you cannot make much from up sells by pricing your product too low.

After all, your income potential will be capped by the small size of the market.

In this case, if your market size is smaller, you will do well to sell your product at a higher prize, maybe $97.00 per copy.

After all, you only need to sell more than 103 copies of your E-Book and make $10,000.00.

Of course, the higher you price your product, the more your customer will be expecting from your product's quality delivery.

Tip: Ending your product price with "7" secures your product at a hot price spot. For examples: $27.00, $37.00, $47.00, $67.00, $97.00, $147.00, $167.00, $247.00, and so on.

Other hot spot prices include: $8.99, $9.95, $14.99, $19.95, $79.00.

3. Title

Thinking of your product's title in advance gives you incredible focus.

And the more relevant your title is to your product's contents, the more memorable it can become to your prospects.

Branding Tip: You can start a franchise/group of products in your name/company name.

This manual and the rest of the Modules of this package are good examples.

So, you've scored a few tips here:

Keep your product name as short and easy to remember as possible (as easy as being able to remember by its initials or short name).

This is optional, but if you want to instill a form of branding, you can include the name of your company/franchise/group of trademarked products.

Alternatively, you can even include your name in the title.

4. **Contents**

Here are some of the most commonly-used content-type formats in the E-Book marketplace (and even in your local bookshops):

How to Guide/Manual - This is by far one of the most popular types of Information Product, even in your local bookshops. This manual is an example of a "How to" product.

Another example you are probably familiar with is the Dummies series. Notice that their titles often come in this format: **[Insert How to Topic] for Dummies**.

Stories - You can present your E-Book contents in story format, or compile a collection of short stories to form an E-Book.

This is recommended for you if you are creative person and a good storyteller in writing.

Tips - Titles such as "100 Tips on How to be a Super Salesperson", "50 Tips on How to Date Women" and "99 Tips for MLM Success" fall under the tips category.

Expect that the reader already has at least minimal understanding on the topic itself.

Directory/Reference - Like a telephone directory, you create a lot of convenience for your readers because you did all the homework in advance.

An example of a directory can be "The Complete Directory of Online Drop Shippers".

Interview - This is for you if you do not have what it takes to chalk out your own content, but know of an expert in a field who is willing to spend some time to be interviewed.

You can record your interview with him or her in both writing (transcript) and audio (audio/video).

5. Font

There are no boundaries for fonts other than using fonts that are readily installed in most PCs around the world.

Some of the best fonts to use are Arial, Times New Roman, Georgia, Verdana, and Courier New.

If you are encouraging your readers to print your E-Book and read, then you are recommended to write your E-Book in Times New Roman (such as this font now), as it is the best-red font in print.

If you are expecting your readers to read your E-Book on their monitors, then writing your material in Arial (Arial) is strongly recommended as it is the best read font on screen.

6. Number of pages

I have taken a survey on an online forum (lucky you), and I have learned that readers in general do expect the number of pages to go in an almost proportion with the price they pay!

For example, if your product is priced at $97.00, readers are expecting more pages of quality information (though not precisely how many, even 70-80 pages are ideal for $97.00 products).

I thought you would also be interested this informal survey's results on PDF vs EXE E-Books:

"If you are to purchase one of the two Info Products, both priced at $30.00 each and of the same quality, one has more pages than the other, which one will you purchase?"

17 members polled for the $30.00 product that has more pages, appreciating elaborate explanation, while 2 other polled for the other one with the least pages, giving the reason that they prefer to absorb what they strictly need to know in the shortest time span.

The results were almost similar when the price of the products changed.

Oh and here's something else I thought you also need to know: any Info Product with about 20 pages or less are usually considered "reports" while others with more than 20 pages are considered "E-Books". :-)

7. **Page size**

Keep your pages in Letter sized – **always**! This is true especially if your customers are mainly from the Western side of the world. Note that their papers are letter-sized.

8. **Format**

PDF! PDF! PDF! And don't ever sell your E-Book(s) in EXE format. Why?

For one, PDF is the best-selling Info Product format in several areas of the Internet marketplace.

Secondly, many computer users prefer PDF E-Books over EXE formatted E-Books for various reasons such as below:

EXE programs often spell a suspicion of computer virus.

Price to price, computer users often value PDF E-Books higher than that of EXE programs.

To be able to create your E-Book in EXE format, you have to have a certain degree of HTML knowledge, which you might or might not have.

This is not the case with using Microsoft Word to create your E-Book as it more user-friendly and most of its functions are pretty much self explanatory.

Macintosh users cannot open EXE programs, thus the E-Book is available only to a smaller market.

While there are not many Macintosh users (I estimated 10% of the prospects are Mc users) in the Internet marketplace, I strongly suggest that you do not exclude these minority users from being your potential customers as some of them do have great buying power.

Given the many reasons above, it is only wise if you would sell your E-Book in PDF format.

9. Affiliate Program links

Again, this is closely associated with your target market and other businesses in the same niche. You want to earn beyond just making up front sales.

You also want to earn more from the same customers by having them purchase more from your recommendations in your E-Book.

One way is to create your own products or membership site, which will obviously consume more of your time and effort (and maybe money).

It will also require more of your expertise, which you might not have.

One other alternative is to join an affiliate program you can recommend in your E-Book for back end income.

For instance, your product can be aimed at a group of people who are interested in cooking oriental dishes.

You can include a recommendation/ad in your E-Book that leads to a membership site for chefs, run by someone else. You merely play your role as an affiliate here.

You get paid for your referral's subscription, and it can be recurring if your affiliate program is a membership/service model!

If there are little affiliate programs available for your market, you either have to start your own or it's a sign that shows how obscure your niche may be.

Creating Your Info Product

I'll be guiding you on creating your Info Product that sells (even if it's your first one) – step by step. Firstly, open your Word Program.

The following is the chronological order of how you should write and organize your Information Product that sells.

Product Cover

Always, always – and always – start your first page with a cover. I am constantly amazed at the number of writers and Info Product authors who create their products without a cover.

Are they from another planet? I don't think I'll ever find out.

But on my planet, we always start our product creation with a cover. We give our "new-born-profit-maker" a face. Care to come to my planet?

You've read this far and there's no way you could miss seeing my product cover earlier, in print or not.

Front Cover

It could be just as good for you if you have and know how to use this powerful Paint program, too, to design your own product cover.

So, if you know how to design your own cover professionally, do just that and paste it into the first page of your Information Product in Word format, like below:

Designer Tips: You can easily source for good, copyright-free images for free and use them in your covers, just as I use them for mine.

I frequent pexels.com and unsplashed.com. I am very much pleased with their wealth of copyright-free images and photos. You will be interested in using them, too.

But if you do not know how to design your own graphic cover well, you can:

1. Use whatever skill you have to create your own cover within the Word Program environment. It can consist of fancy-styled titles, wordings, boxes, and more. (See example in the next page)

2. Alternatively, if you have the money to spare, you can engage a graphic designer to do the work for you.

Example cover designed in Word environment

101
Easy Ways
To Get Out of Debt

By [Debt-Free Guru]

Discover the *Little* Known Ways on How You Can *Get Out* of Your Debt <u>Legally and Easily</u>!

Important: To receive lifetime updates on this manual, Please subscribe to my mailing list <u>here</u>.

www.[sitename].com

Usually, the graphic designer you hire to create the cover for you also designs the product image for it (also known as "E-Cover").

Here are examples of an E-Cover:

If you aren't keen on hiring a graphic designer to create the E-Cover for you, you can still create your own one automatically with software from Virtual Cover Creators.

The importance of a good E-Cover in your sales letter will be covered in detail in Module #2 of this series.

Important Notices

On the second page of your E-Book is where you should state your copyright, legal and/or guarantee notices (simply refer to Page 2 of this manual for an example of how your copyright/legal/guarantee notice can be written).

A very important thing to note to your reader on the same page (or the next) is that if your reader has any form of **Resell Rights** or **Give Away Rights** to your product.

Again, if you would read the second page of this manual:

> **Important Rights Notice** (Sample)
>
> This is **NOT** a free E-Book. Thus, this E-Book may **NOT** be sold or given away either in part or full under any circumstances. To do so would be a breach of copyright. Only the Publisher and authorized resellers have the right to resell this package subject to the terms and conditions given.

So, if you have decided that you are the only one to sell your own product and not convey any form of Resell Rights, you may write your rights notice like below:

This E-Book cannot be sold or given away or free. Only the Publisher has the right to sell this product (package).

If you are also going to sell the Basic Resell Rights to a limited number of resellers, then you may write your rights notice like the following:

Only the Publisher and his authorized resellers have the right to resell this product (package).

If you are conveying Master Resell Rights to your product, which means anyone who has the product can choose to resell the product and keep all the profits:

You now have Master Resell Rights to this product. You may resell this product at $20.00 (suggested price) and keep all the profits.

This product cannot be given away for free. However, this product can be added to a paid membership site, bundled into a paid package, or be given away as a bonus to another product you are selling.

Table of Contents

Now, here's what usually follows your notices – your table of contents.

You want to have your reader get a sneak peak at your product's contents at a glance – all in one page/section.

Your table of contents can be formatted like the following:

Table of Contents

Introduction	4
Title #1	7
Title #2	15
Title #3	21
Title #4	28

Tip: If your product has several topics and pages, you can give your readers a lot of reading convenience (if they are reading on the computer) by hyper-linking your topics in the table of contents.

This way, your reader only has to click on a chosen topic in the table of contents to get to the page rather than scroll down to its page, especially if it's in the 100-200 page range.

Here's how you can hyper-link the topics in your table of contents, step-by-step:

1. Compile your product in full.

2. Starting with the first chapter, you need to put your cursor blink in front of the topic's title. Insert bookmark and give the bookmark a name, say, '1stchapter'.

3. Go to your "Table of Contents" page and highlight the entire line of the topic indicated with your cursor (in this case, the first chapter of your product).

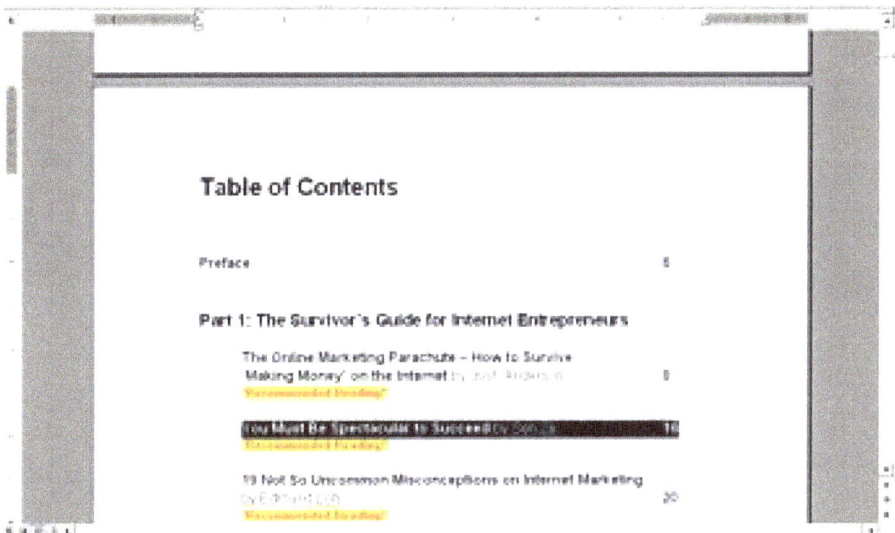

4. And then, right-click on the text (or CTRL-K in short). A drop-down menu will appear, and select "Hyperlink". Another window appears.

5. On your left hand of the menu, select "Place in the Document".

Select the name of the bookmark ('1stchapter' in the example), and click OK.

6. The link is now associated. Notice the link has changed to blue and is now clickable when you do a CTRL-click action on it and it will bring you to the page where you bookmarked earlier.

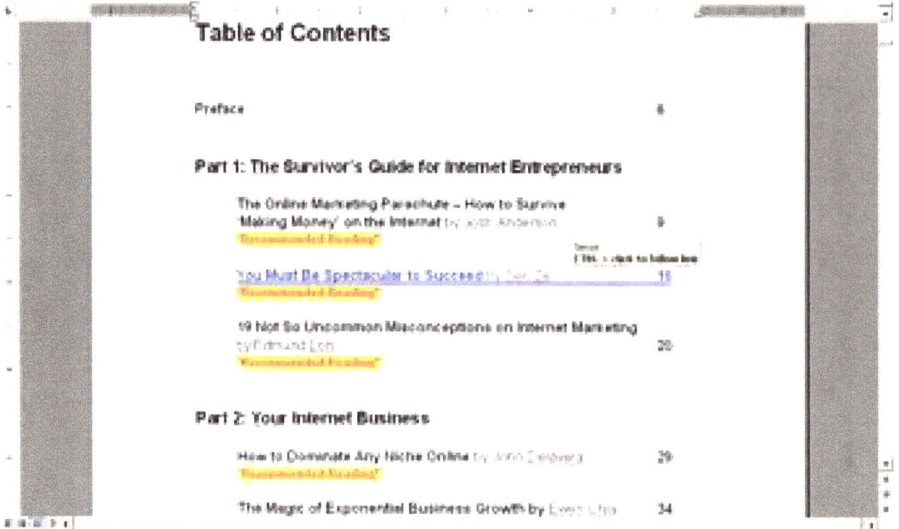

7. In order to remove the underline style, highlight the text and click CTRL-U. To change the color of the text to black or any other colors of your choice, simply highlight the text and change using your Font Color function (see below your MS Word program).

Finally, your reader can now jump around at every parts of your Info Product simply by you enabling them to click on the topic links in the table of contents to get him there!

Page Layout

One word of advice: always keep your page layout WHITE! You're not offering a Power Point presentation for sale. Instead, you should be taking into consideration about how much ink your reader will need to print your product out.

Some of your readers are probably treasuring the amount of ink they have left in their cartridge box. Thus, make sure when they have to "spend" their ink, it'd be worth every dot.

One way is to just keep your page layout white (like what you're reading on now). No black, no red, and no pictures of an expensive car.

After all, people purchase E-Books for information, not for the sake of seeing expensive cars in the background overlaid by text.

And about your page size, I've said it earlier but it bears repeating: keep it **letter-sized**. You already know why, if you've been following me up until now.

Now, let's talk about your page header and footer (the one at the top and bottom of your page).

You can easily create your own header and footer by going to **View -> Header and Footer**.

You want to create another form of branding here as well.

Since it is very likely that your reader will print out your Info Product to read, you may want to include your name, product title, and even your web site URL in every page's header and footer, such as what you're seeing on this page now.

(I told you that you're looking at the best Info Product example?)

Contents

Now, here comes the heart of the product – **content!**

Regardless of what type of information you will be dispensing in your paid E-Book, it must the following criteria:

- ✓ Saves time,
- ✓ Saves money,
- ✓ Saves effort,
- ✓ Makes money (optional),
- ✓ Solves problems, and
- ✓ Gives benefits.

As you can see, without one or more of the above requirements, your information wouldn't amount to quality worth paying for.

Examples:

- **"How to Play Golf Professionally in 13 Days"**

Isn't $30.00 worth paying for since the information within this manual can help you achieve professional peak in 13 days? Or would you rather take forever?

- **"How to Make Money Online"**

For only $97.00, you can now make money online. Or would you rather save $97.00 and make mistakes that amount more than that?

- **"How to Prevent Your Divorce"**

Is $67.00 too much to ask from your wallet or do you prefer to let go of your spouse and pay at least 50% in assets after the divorce is granted by the court?

Here are ways you can compile quality, in-demand content, paid or free:

1. **Write on Your Own**

Personally, this is my best preferred way of creating content, though I can't possibly say that this is for everyone, too.

Creative people often say that it's a way to show how much you know or what an expert you are in a certain field, but I prefer to sum it up as, "I didn't waste my last 20 years of my life."

Writing your own content gives you more authority over your own content alongside with giving your own insights, expert opinions and recommendations, which can be more powerful than any other methods of content creation.

Writing own content can be a fear for others, somehow, and they often hide behind the excuse that "they don't know much".

If you are one of them, I'd like to remind you that you're probably looking down on yourself, or that you are, in a way, saying, "I wasn't really doing anything productive for my last lifetime."

In short, writing on your own also requires self-esteem in your vast wealth of knowledge. The downside, though, is that this method requires a lot of time and effort on your part, not just the expertise and ability to write well.

2. Interview

Now, if you are truly exploring a market where you know nothing of other than the fact it IS profitable, here's one sure fire way: **interview an expert!**

Whether you've been living a life of "jack of all trades" or know nothing about that market, interviewing an expert on the subject not only saves you from grave danger of knowing nothing, but you can have your content churned out by someone else more capable.

It can be done free, in most cases! It need not be someone who goes online. In fact, you can interview a friend or someone you know who is an expert in a field where people are willing to pay (or even die for, in extreme cases).

Your product's value can be tremendously added if you can get the interviewee to transcribe his or her information in audio format as well as text (transcript).

3. Hire a Ghost Writer

This one requires you to invest your sum of money, but you get to save your other valuable assets: **time and effort**.

If you are horrible at writing, don't know the topic well enough to write it for sale and know no one to be an expert in it, this can be your best method in churning out quality content.

A ghost writer, in a nutshell, is someone who does the writing without taking any credit. Obviously, it's nothing to do with the ghosts you're probably thinking of right now.

You can go to eLance.com, bid and engage a ghostwriter of your choice. You can get one or more ghostwriters to write the content for you in several articles. The last time I recall, you can get one to write a 300-400 word article at $5.00 each.

It's up to the ghostwriters to do the research on the topic.

Once you have them written the contents in many articles, you can proof-read them, edit, and later compile them into a paid Info Product for sale.

4. **Public Domain**

If you're not familiar with the term "public domain" allow me to help give you at least a general idea of the legal and business power contained in these two words.

At a very basic level, "public domain" means "anything that is NOT protected under US copyright law".

This includes ALL works published before 1923 and, under certain conditions, works published up to 1978.

A 'work' can be anything: a book, a play, music, photographs, movies, instruction manuals, courses, reports, posters, and more.

Of course, we're now referring to books, courses, reports, and manuals for this purpose.

Republishing and repackaging public domain information and other creative works can make you a lot of money other than saving you time from writing your own quality content.

The reason is fairly simple: If you find, re-package and sell information that has fallen into the public domain, you don't have to pay royalties or copyright fees on that work.

If you love the idea of publishing information as a business model but you don't want to or can't create your own book or manual, this method is for you.

Not every kind of work in the public domain will have a market but here are some examples of books you could be republishing that have an excellent market demand right now:

- Mind reading
- Marketing
- Advertising
- Copywriting
- Trading stocks and commodities
- Hobbies
- Arts
- Crafts
- Herb remedies
- Natural healing

- Children stories etc.

More information on public domain:

http://www.E-Book-business.com/publicdomain.php

A Word on Free Articles

As you can see, compiling free articles didn't make the list. For one, they don't represent quality information, as usually the purpose of articles is introducing the surface of a certain topic.

Secondly, if you would study the reprint right terms and conditions for article directories such as eZinearticles.com, you will learn that you are not allowed to compile any one article for sale, even if you credit the author by republishing his or her resource box.

Joining Affiliate Programs

Here's an advantage that conventional books don't have – a convenient way to earn more from the sales of your E-Books!

And you can do so by joining affiliate programs and endorse them in your E-Book.

> **Affiliate and Affiliate Program Explained**
>
> If you're not familiar with these Internet Marketing terms yet, here's a brief explanation:
>
> **Affiliate** – one who acts as a referrer to pre-sell/recommend products or services of a company/business and receives commission on every successful sale.
>
> **Affiliate Program** – a program that provides a system where it allows affiliates to sign up and pre-sell/recommend products or services of a company/business for commissions.

Let's face it – you cannot possibly earn even a comfortable living selling just once to one customer.

And regardless of how big or small the size of the market you are catering to, you will definitely tire yourself fast by selling one product once to one customer.

Thus, the wisest way to do business in the information market is to **create repeat customers**. And recommending products and/or services you are affiliated with is the way to go.

Given the brief explanations above, it would be even better if you recommend quality services (such as membership sites) you are affiliated with to your readers via your E-Book contents because through that method, you can earn income every month!

Affiliate programs that offer recurring commissions include membership sites, services, matrixes, multi level marketing (MLM), and 2-tiers.

First, you sign up for at least one affiliate program (preferably more than one). Once you have configured your important details such as your personal details, method of receiving payment, and more, extract your affiliate ID and include it in your E-Book in a form of recommendation or advertisement.

Affiliate Program Success Choice Factors

1. **Demand**

I have discussed about researching on the demand earlier in this manual. If you have chosen a profitable market to capitalize, you will be sure that there is an abundance of affiliate programs to choose from.

2. **Commission incentive**

Forget affiliate programs that pay you 5% to 20%. Out of the affiliate programs you are prospecting, you will do well to narrow down your search to those that pays a minimum of 40% to 50% per product/service sale.

Preferably, you join at least one affiliate program that pays on a recurring basis.

3. Sales letter conversion rate

One of the best ways to tell if a sales letter is written persuasively or not is to read it yourself. If you don't feel persuaded to buy, then it is likely that many others will not, either.

Your referral efforts can be a waste if the principal's sales letter doesn't convert well.

This is because no matter how many people you refer to the sales page as an affiliate, very few of them will go on to be customers, if any at all, regardless of how great the product or service can be.

4. Promotion materials

One of the main ideas of becoming an affiliate is to do less work while making more money.

Of course, an affiliate program has already saved you tremendous time and effort (and maybe money) from having to create your own product or service.

However, you would also want to do less work where ad-writing is concerned. You should expect the affiliate program to provide necessary promotion materials such as banners, solo ads, endorsement letters, and more.

5. Quality

While this is self explanatory, you can gain a tremendous edge in your endorsements by relating your personal experience and benefits from the program you have tested out yourself.

Best Places to Source for Affiliate Programs

http://www.associateprograms.com/

http://paydotcom.com/

http://www.clickbank.com/

http://www.lifetimecommissions.com/

http://www.2-tier.com/

http://www.linkshare.com/

http://www.affiliatefirst.com/

http://www.refer-it.com/

Cloaking Your Affiliate ID

You can easily shorten your affiliate links and keep them neat and easy to remember, which can be lengthy at times by cloaking them.

Another benefit of doing so is that in case of URL changes made by the principal, you can easily customize your redirecting URL to point to the changed affiliate link.

Recommended URL redirection/cloaking service:

http://www.findv.com/

http://www.graburl.com/

Info Product Creation Tips

1. Writing an E-Book from A to Z can be long and tiring, especially if there are many pages in your Info Product. You can first write different topics and articles of your E-Book (even in no particular order), save them in a folder, and later compile them into one final product.

2. When writing, assume you are writing to ONE person only. Since you've read up until now, you are certain that I am addressing this entire information to YOU, not a "gang" or "everyone". In short, write in terms of "you" and "me".

3. There is a certain degree to the truth that most Information Products are repackaged and republished. What adds value to a product that sells is branding and personalization. You can easily do so by relating your expert insights, opinions and strategies of your own, if any.

4. If there is any need for you to do a word count, you can easily discover how many words have been written into your product by going to **Tools -> Word Count**. This is especially important if you are selling the Private Label Rights to your Information Product or articles by any chance.

5. Once your product is converted into PDF format, you cannot change it anymore. Your product cannot be changed especially when it comes into the hands of your customers. Thus, you will do well to proof-read your product at least twice before declaring it a "completed product". That way, you will reduce less mistakes, errors and omissions in your product. You can easily proof-read and check for spelling mistakes by pressing F7 to perform a "Spell Check".

6. Due to the often changing nature of the Internet, the information within your product can be obsolete given time. You can easily update your customers on new versions of your Info Product by having them subscribed to your mailing list for life time updates at your Thank You Page, or in the product itself.

7. Remember to disable the copying function when converting your Word document into PDF format! You won't want to make content copying convenient for content thieves when all they have to do is press CTRL-A, followed by CTRL-C on your product!

8. Always keep your Word document and don't delete it even if you have a knack to clear files off your hard drive. It can be worth 5-10 times the price of your usual product.

9. You can make reading convenient for your readers by stressing out important texts in some parts of your product even with a simple "bold", "italic", "underline", or "highlight" feature.

10. Last but not least, remember that your Info Product for sale has 3 purposes: make money for you <u>upfront</u>, make **more** money for you <u>back-end</u>, and **collect quality leads**!

In Closing

There you go! You are now fully equipped with the step-by-step "know how" of creating an Info Product that sells out of thin air!

And with this knowledge put into practice, you can create countless Info Products of your own – your imagination is the limit.

But that's **not** all to the entire picture of making money online from your paperless E-Book publishing. Read Module #2 of the Info Product Empire package now and let's find out how you can get all dressed up for Online Business!

I'll see you there!

Recommended Resources

Recommended Reading

[Edmund Loh's 8 Profit-Pulling PLR Strategies That Really Work!](#) – unlock the secrets to making money with Private Label Rights using 8 totally unique, killer strategies!

[19 Internet Business Models](#) – eliminate guesswork and discover what makes the world go round for Internet Entrepreneurs and copy their success business systems for your own in a flash – low cost, high profit!

All-in-One E-Commerce Solutions

[SOLOBIS](#) – all-in-one solution comes with unlimited web hosting, domain name, unlimited auto responders, broadcast feature, custom web builder, file manager, link cloakers, JV manager, 500+ beautiful web templates, online support team, and many more. No HTML and programming knowledge required.

Recommended Payment Processors

[2CheckOut.com](#) – start accepting credit card payments from customers from several parts of the world!

Module 2: Info Product Business Setup Explained

Having a business system that works is one of the **most important Internet Marketing success factors**, and I will be dedicating this sequel to showing you, **step-by-step**, on how you can create your Internet Business following 3 slightly-deferred-but-proven blueprints I have discovered – the proven and tested blueprint used by **top** Internet Marketers today.

Always **was**, always **is**, and always **will**.

Just to let you have a *rough* idea of the type of system you are going to construct from this blueprint, a top Internet Entrepreneur whom I had the privilege to study after used one blueprint and sold <u>more than 3,000 copies</u> of his $97 E-Books on the Internet in the space of 2 years.

That works up to more than **$291,000**, which also works up to more than **$145,000 a year**.

Another entrepreneur used another deferred blueprint, but his results were almost just as amazing, especially when we talk about <u>**residual income**</u> from his leads service (you'll get to see him in the case study later).

Don't let the figures intimidate you but I want you to realize the **power and value** of the information you now have in your hands.

This manual is **NOT** solely about copywriting, though I will be covering some basic principles of writing a sales letter that works. You can't make money without knowing and putting them into practice.

You won't find me recommending *expensive* professional services to overcome whatever disabilities you may have because I will show you how you can do everything yourself and where to get all the things you need to get started for *free* or *dirt-cheap* fees regardless of whether you have a flair for writing or not, have any programming or designing skills or not.

It doesn't matter if this is your first time in business and it works in any field or niche.

Game for Round Two?

To Your Paperless E-Book Publishing Success!

The 3 Business Models You Can Choose From

First thing's first: there are only **two** main purposes of your web site. They are:

- To sell your product to your customer
- Capture leads.

That's all. Yet, these simplified purposes are often overlooked by most Internet Marketers.

Your site isn't there to have many links and contents. Your site isn't there to give freebies (you can't get rich that way, anyway).

Your web site only sells your product and capture leads. **It is that simple**.

This is especially true since you will only be selling at least one Information Product (also known as digital product) off your web site.

In a conventional sense, you are setting up a mini-shop, not a supermarket, which sells only one product or a group of products of the same theme.

A marketing school of thought says that you **either go small or go big**.

In other words, there is a razor edge between starting a small Internet Business as compared to a huge Internet Business, like Amazon.com.

Now, there is **nothing wrong** with a smaller size of an Internet Business, such as what I am about to reveal to you in the coming pages.

If you are running an online version of "Wal-Mart", your prospects are likely to expect you to have everything under the sun and if you cannot start an Online

Business that size, you are better off starting a business that sells only one product.

Your site becomes more prospect-focused, and your prospects on the other hand are ready to expect what you have to offer.

Having said that, many beginning Internet Marketers are not clear with the major goals thus their lack of focus often shows on their web sites.

Well, that's **not** going to happen to you, not with this manual in your hands, as far as I am concerned!

There are **3** ways you can structure your business system (or school of thoughts, if you would like to call them) and achieve the two goals stated earlier, which are selling to your prospects and collecting subscriber leads.

Given no specific name, here are the 3 ways you can model your business system:

1. Model A

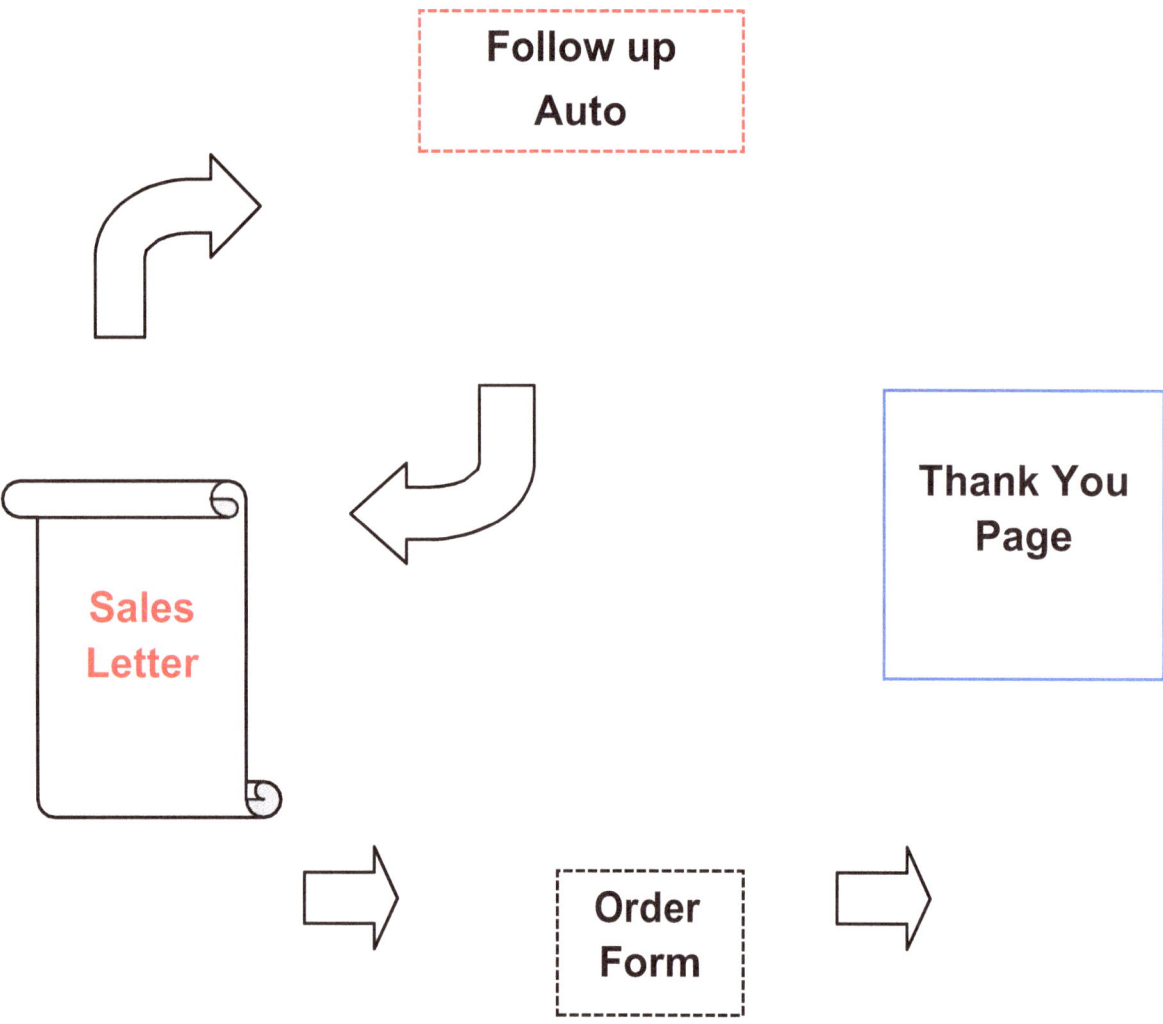

The concept is simple. You set up a well-written and persuasive one-page sales letter on your web site.

The only thing your prospect is going to see at your web site is your sales letter but there is more to it than meets the eye.

Your sales letter does all the selling to persuade your potential customer to buy your product from you.

There are <u>no other links</u> on your sales letter aside from your **Buy Button**. If your prospect is interested in your product, he will buy from you.

Your prospect, now your customer, will proceed to your order form and pays you with his credit card via a credit card payment processor you have set up in your order form.

Since your product is digital in nature, your customer will then be redirected to your Thank You Page you have created where he can download your product.

This process can be automated and very often, your net profit is very <u>close to 100%</u>.

There are transaction and deduction fees incurred by your credit card payment processor but they are so small they can be negligible.

If your prospect decides NOT to buy from you, you install a script in your sales letter to have a small window pop up when your prospect leaves your web page.

In the pop up window, you ask for your prospect's permission to leave his name and e-mail address for you to follow-up with him using an auto responder.

Earlier, you have written your series of follow-up messages to be e-mailed to your prospects on intervals and if your prospect leaves his name and e-mail address, your auto responder can do the follow-up on your part, automatically, sparing you the manual work which can be non-productive.

In your follow-up series, you reveal extra information or maybe give a sample of your product but the objective is the same: to **persuade** your prospect to buy from **YOU**.

Most people don't buy on first contact and when they leave your web site, chances are they will forget where they were 10 web pages ago.

And if you fail to persuade your prospect to be your customer after a few follow-up messages, you can invite your prospect to be your affiliate and partner in success.

If your prospect becomes your affiliate by signing up for your affiliate program, he will promote your product to his network of contacts for a commission. **And the cycle continues**.

Examples of this Business Model

Guide to Private Label Rights

http://www.ebizmodelsyoucancopy.com/plc

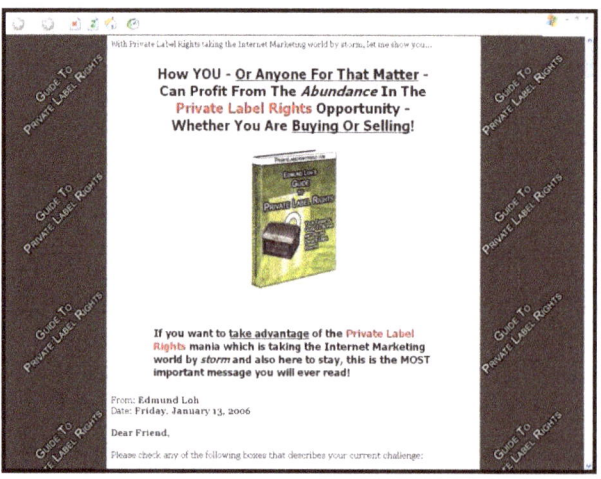

My Seduction Secrets

http://www.myseductionsecrets.com/

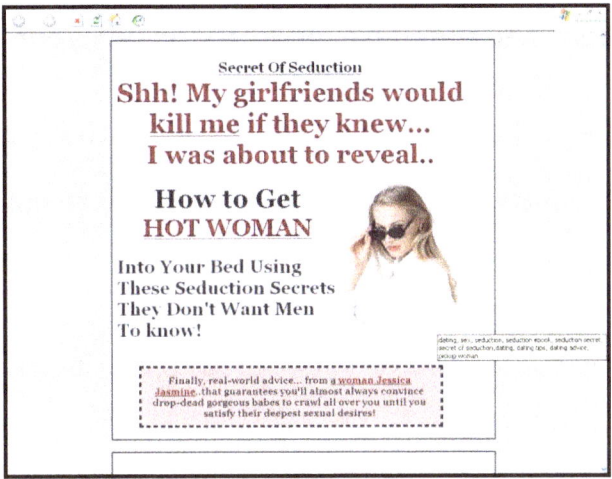

2. Model B

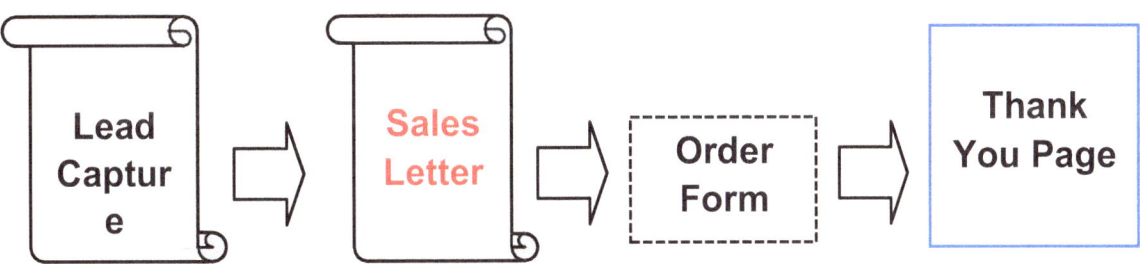

Contrary to the first model, you capture the prospect's name and email address <u>FIRST</u>.

On the lead capture page, you provide information on what the prospect should be expecting from you, in a nutshell.

Once he or she is interested and enters his name and email address into your opt in form, he or she will be directed to your sales letter.

The rest of the process here is similar to Model A, where your prospect reads your sales letter and if he or she is convinced and interested, he or she will go on to be your customer and purchase your product via your Order Form.

The difference between this model and the former is that you capture your prospect's lead first, which if done right; you are likely to collect more leads as compared to Model A.

He or she will then be subscribed to your auto responder mailing list where he or she will receive follow up letters from you in effort to persuade him or her to purchase your product by providing extra useful information NOT found in your sales letter.

The advantage of doing this model is that even if your prospect, who opted into your mailing list, can be followed up with other products or services you either own or are an affiliate for, regardless of whether he purchases your primary product or not.

Examples of this Business Model

Megapreneur Millions System

http://www.megapreneurmillions.com/

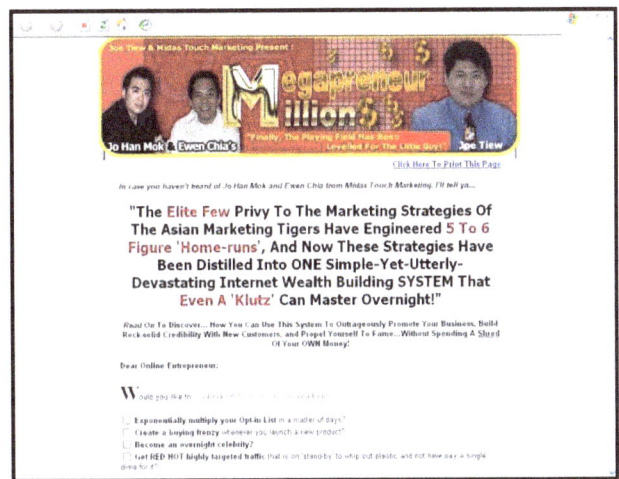

List Builder Pro

http://www.listbuilderpro.com/

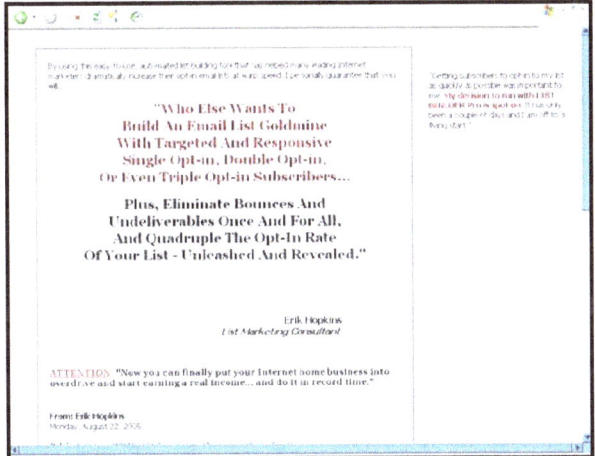

3. Model C

This one is slightly tricky to do and requires a certain degree of good copywriting skills.

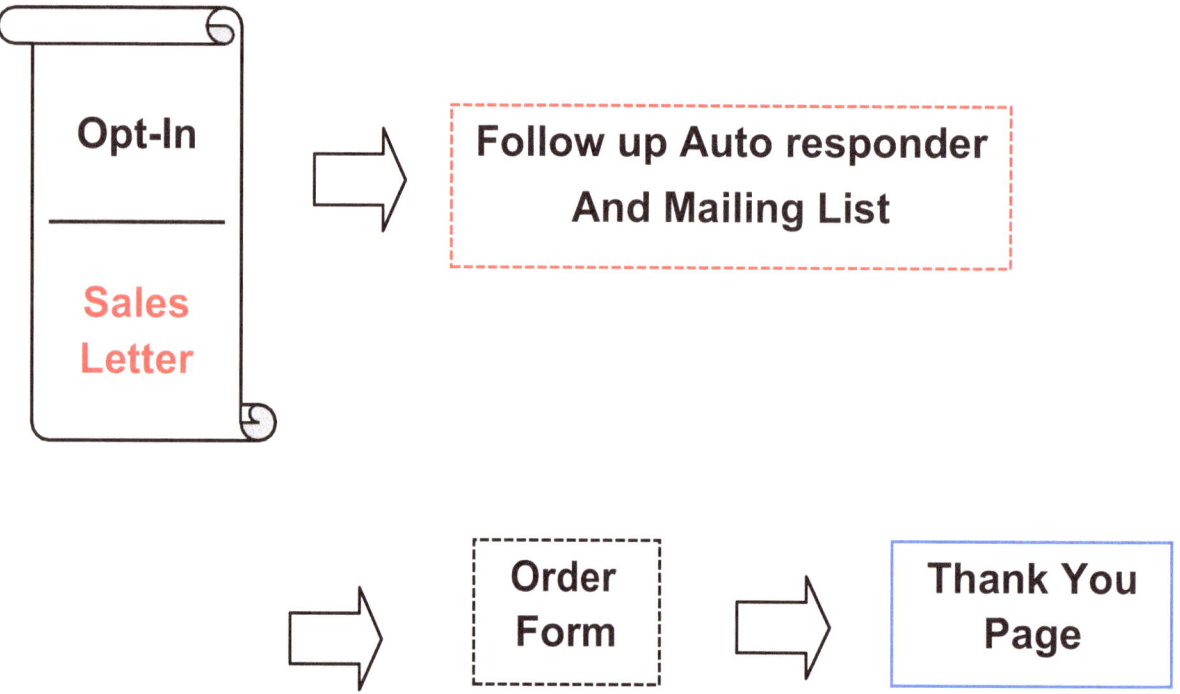

In the letter itself, the first component (top) is aimed at <u>capturing the subscriber's name and email address</u> to be subscribed to your mailing list whereas the second component (bottom) is aimed at <u>selling your product to your prospect</u>.

As far as my observation concludes, this is the <u>least used</u> model of all the 3 models.

The rest of the process is similar to Models A and B, but you would require a certain degree of good copywriting skills to follow this particular model successfully.

This is because on the letter itself, you want to convince your prospect to subscribe to your mailing list first, and later be redirected back to this same letter.

As far as the next battle to profits is concerned, you now want to persuade your prospect to buy your product now. This is probably the hardest to do of all models. But given the 3 choices, you can decide which one works best for you.

What You Need

1. **Domain name**

This is your web site address (e.g. www.yourdomain.com).

Recommended domain names:

http://www.godaddy.com/

http://www.namecheap.com/

2. **Web hosting**

You need web space where you store your files and documents such as web pages, scripts and images.

Recommended web hosting:

http://www.sitehost4u.com/

http://www.doteasy.com/

3. Auto responder

A follow-up system that can automatically follow-up with your prospects after they leave your web page.

Most of the time, people don't buy on first contact.

Therefore, having an auto responder is essential for your Internet Business for follow up purposes until you are able to convert some more of your prospects into customers.

Recommended auto responders:

http://www.freeautobot.com/ (free service)

http://www.getresponse.com/

http://www.aweber.com/ (paid service, recommended)

4. Credit card payment processor

It enables your customer to pay you with credit card through a secure server.

Recommended processors:

http://www.2checkout.com/

http://www.paypal.com/

5. Affiliate program

It is your marketing life wire. You have to leverage on other people's marketing efforts to sell your product on your behalf.

Recommended affiliate program:

http://paydotcom.com/

(free to setup, $29 for premier account)

http://www.clickbank.com/

6. **Other Tools**

- **FTP program** - I use WS FTP Pro to upload my files to my web host server.

- **HTML editor** - I use Macromedia Dreamweaver to create HTML documents.

- **Paint program** - You will need to use a professional paint program to edit and create images for your sales letter and E-Cover. I use Adobe Photoshop.

Recommended Resource for Those Who Do Not Have HTML, Designing and/or Programming Skills

You can get all of your Internet Business necessities such as domain name, web hosting, auto responder, PDF converter, file upload manager, web site builder, sales letter generator, pop-up generator, and more at **SOLOBIS** for a low monthly fee.

This way, you can save money from purchasing tools ala carte and time and effort sourcing for them. You are not required to have any experience in programming and designing either to access this suite.

Writing Your Sales Letter

This chapter will be long – and **the most important** as well. I cannot cover every ground on copywriting in this manual alone, but I'll show you the important aspects of creating a copy that sells.

Regardless of which of the 3 models you choose, the ability to write a persuasive sales letter is not optional, which is why I am dedicating this entire chapter to writing your sales letter.

The good news is that this is only a one-time activity and you won't need to repeat it again! It's a system, remember? It's supposed to be taking care of your boring chores!

The other good news is that like anything else, it requires nothing more than practice and testing your sales letter conversion rate and results.

In the next page, I detail to you a draft format of what your sales letter should be like in a nutshell.

You will discover that what works offline works online, too. In this case, you are taking a **direct response piece** to cyber space.

The Format of Your Sales Letter

YOUR HEADLINE HERE

> FIX PRODUCT IMAGE HERE

YOUR SUB-HEADLINE HERE
Write a summary of your product

INTRODUCE YOURSELF
Tell a little about yourself, what you do and how you can solve your prospect's problem through your product or service you are offering

EXPLAIN THE BENEFITS AND FEATURES OF YOUR PRODUCT
in a neat, presentable and tabled form

TESTIMONIALS
of happy customers, top names, and endorsements to your product to explain the results your customers will get as a result of using your product

BONUSES (OPTIONAL)
as incentives for your prospects to buy from you

PERSUADE TO BUY NOW
include money-back guarantee statement, your order form and a persuasive summary to prone your prospects to take action now

Privacy | Disclaimer | Affiliate Program

The diagram above is a draft format of what your sales letter should look like.

Layout

Your main text color should be **black** on a **white** background.

You can have other colors such as blue, red and gray on your website, but the background behind the text should be white.

The color of your main text should be black. **No other exceptions**! That is because this is the **easiest format to read**. You are in business so dress your site in a business manner.

Any Other Links?

Besides the link to the **Pay button**, there should be <u>**no other links on your sales letter**</u>. This is an important key to success for this blueprint. That means no links to About Me, F.A.Q., and Sitemap.

You shouldn't put any advertisements (banner ads, Google Adsense and the likes) on your sales letter, either. You don't want to *distract* your prospect.

You want him to **stay focused** – and continue reading your sales letter from *top* to *bottom*.

Therefore, you have to explain who you are, what you do, and how you can help your prospect to solve his problems – **all in one page**.

This can result in writing a long sales letter. You might wonder if your prospect will actually read your lengthy sales letter.

That depends a lot on how **well-written** your sales letter is and **how interested your prospect is** in your product.

These links can be exceptional, however:

- **Disclaimer and Privacy pages**. If your prospect needs to see these pages, try either putting them on the same page as the sales letter or open them in a new window. That way, your prospect will not get distracted from reading your sales letter.

You can get a disclaimer page for free here.

- **Your contact e-mail address**. Should your prospect have any questions, this information is essential to put into your sales letter. However, you are advised **NOT** to hyperlink it as it can be a SPAM-magnet as there countless automatic spam-blasters creeping in cyberspace! Instead, just write your e-mail address as it is. Preferably, write your e-mail address in this format: **yourname[at]emailaddress.com** instead of yourname@emailaddress.com.

- **A link to signing up for your affiliate program**. A big number of the prospects who visit your sales letter will not likely buy your product. However, you can convert some of the non-buyers to be your affiliates and sell on your part to earn commissions.

With no other links in your sales letter, it boils down ultimately to whether your prospect **buys from you or not**.

Fonts

You should use fonts that are availably ready in all PCs. Arial is the easiest font to read on the computer screen so you are encouraged to use this font.

Other fonts such as Times New Roman, Georgia, Verdana, Tahoma, and Courier New are also commonly-used fonts for effective sales letters.

Do not use *uncommon* fonts.

This is because not all PCs can recognize such *bizarre* fonts you are using for your sales letter, making your prospect see something else that appears otherwise on his computer screen thus damaging the impression and the looks of your sales letter.

Now, let's go work on your first sales letter. ;-)

The Headline and Sub-headline

This is a *hard and fast* rule. Your sales letter **must have a headline**. That's the first thing your prospects are going to look at when they visit your web site.

Not having a headline is like looking at a headless person! Embarrassingly enough, this is what you often don't see on a big percentage of web sites.

Your headline serves as an advertisement to your prospects. Your headline must grab the attention of your visitors or else they will not read the rest of your sales letter.

This is very crucial – the headline will **make or break** your sales letter!

The size of your headline should be bigger than the rest of the text in your sales letter.

You may want to color and stylize (e.g. <u>underline</u>, **bold**, *italic*, ==highlight==, and ~~strike-through~~) your headline text.

Case Study: Ancient Secrets to Asthma Cure

This is the headline and sub-headline of a sales letter I've made for a client some time ago. My client plans to sell an E-Book on ancient secrets to asthma cure.

His target market is, of course, asthmatic people. After a careful research, he discovers that there is a market looking for a cure on asthma.

And according to his study, about 300 million people world wide are suffering from asthma and it seems that the asthmatics are even hooking onto the Internet in search for a cure.

My client was an ex-asthmatic and has plenty of quality information that he has used to cure his asthma. Now, he's ready to <u>bank</u> on it! ;-)

> **Now At Your Finger Tips**! A Guide To **Asthma Cure** That Reveals Cutting-*Edge* Techniques, Exercises, Tips and Remedies Never Heard Of Before That <u>Can **Save** You From Expensive Medical Bills</u>!

If his prospects are asthmatics or know of anyone who is suffering from this disease and they visit his sales letter, they would definitely stop to read on and learn more about his product and how it can solve their health problems.

Notice that the fonts are big and stylized.

The sub-headline will encourage his prospects to read further:

> **At last, the truth will be unveiled in 212 power-packed letter-sized pages, PDF Format, so that YOU can *CURE* your asthma and get your breath back <u>in the comfort of your own home</u>!**

Now, put yourself in the shoes of an asthmatic person. You are spending too much money on medical bills but your health never improves.

You still suffer from tight breathing and wheeze every night. And the next day, the doctor recommends you to pump the red inhaler!

If you are to see this headline, you'd definitely read with interest. You have never heard of this before.

You badly want to save in medical bills since they never help you improve your health but just increase your stress in finding the money to pay for something that never works.

The sub-headline will give a spark of hope to you who are coughing your life away while frantically searching for a cure – and you have finally found it!

Since you are already interested in reading the sales letter, you will continue reading on.

The rest of your sales letter will tell you about the benefits and features of the product, testimonials from happy customers, who are ex-asthmatics in this case, guarantees, and most importantly, the pay button with a price tag to it.

Would you buy if you are in the shoes of an asthmatic person? Sure, you do. **You are ready to fire the doctor and draw your credit card out**!

So, the **bottom-line** is to start your sales letter with a *compelling* headline followed by a *powerful* summary in the sub-headline.

Long Sales Letter vs. Short Sales Letter?

Now, we have come to an **age-old question** in writing your sales letter:

Is writing long sales letter better than writing a short one – or vice-versa

You don't have to guess. The answer is: **The <u>long</u> sales letter**. Before I tell you why, here's a simple analogy I want to share with you:

I am sure you have watched movies. Some movies run for a long time and others short.

When you watch a short but boring movie, you thank God the show was over in a breeze.

When you watch a short but exciting movie, you wish the movie would run longer, wouldn't you?

When you watch a long but slow and boring movie, you would be in deep agony that you may as well leave the cinema.

See the logic I am trying to tell you? Now do I need to tell you how you would feel about the movie if it was long and exciting?

That's the secret. Write a long and exciting sales letter. Don't just bore your prospect with the features of your product.

Tell him what is in it for him. Don't just write from the perspective of a salesman or even a CEO for that matter.

Write from the perspective of a movie director! It doesn't matter even if you have not been one before.

Just imagine yourself producing a show for your viewers. Just how would you produce a 2 hour movie and keep your viewers watching your show with interest from start to end?

I also believe this is the same secret movie directors use to produce sequels to their initial blockbusters to keep the same viewers to watch!

On the same context, produce an exciting sales letter that keeps your prospect to read from start to end.

And if they like it, they will definitely look forward to another product from yours truly.

This same secret will make back-selling easy. Make him see a good future he can get with the help of your product.

Think in this logic and you will be on the right track. It did very well for successful movie directors and copywriters, so why should you be an exception?

Now, are you still thinking of writing a short sales letter? Don't even think about it! Besides, you're writing a sales letter, not a *brochure*.

A brochure only informs your prospect about the features of your product. It does not sell. Your sales letter **does**.

Benefits vs. Features

Copywriting 101, Part 3:

What happens when you don't explain the benefits of your product in your sales letter?

Answer: **No sales**!

That's right. You don't have to be a copywriter by training to know that.

But somehow, most of us make this terrible mistake, probably because this is so over-simplified we tend to overlook it.

More often that not, **features are often being mistaken as benefits**. If I were in the shoes of a potential customer, I am more interested in **how a product can benefit me**.

Recall the last time you bought a product, online or offline.

Why did you buy it? Did you buy it <u>because of its features</u>? Or did you buy it because <u>it can benefit you or solve your problem</u>?

To learn the distinct **definitions** of benefit and feature, see below:

- [Benefit]. According to the Pocket English Dictionary's definition, it means an *advantage; to be useful or profitable to*. In the case of selling your product on your web page, you want to tell how useful or how your product can solve your prospect's problems.

- [Feature]. According to the Pocket English Dictionary's definition, it means *characteristic*. In the case of selling your product on your web page, you want to also tell your prospect in what form your product is (digital or physical).

Examples of Benefits and Features That You Can Use In Your Sales Letter

- You sell **slimming powder** on your web page (physical product). The feature of your product is **easy-to-digest powder packed in a tin or carton**. The benefit of your product is that consumers **can now lose weight the easy way**!

- You sell **turtle pellets** on your web page (physical product). The feature of your product is **small and easy-to-digest green pellets** for your pet amphibians. The benefit of your product is that it is **easy for your pet amphibians to consume and grow healthily because they are going to get all the nutrition they can get in the pellets**!

- You sell an **information product** on your web page (digital product). The features of your product are **.PDF format** and **have Master Resell Rights**. Therefore, the benefits are your customers **can download it instantly** as soon as they pay and they have an **income opportunity to make money and keep all the profits to themselves**!

All in all, write <u>BOTH</u> features and benefits of your product. Remember to *sell a solution, not a product*!

I know you are cringing when you hear this.

All these while I've been talking about your product and selling it but remember, nobody on this planet buys a product *for the sake of buying a product*!

You buy a product for the sake of *getting the benefits* or *solving your problems* for that matter.

You didn't buy a refrigerator because it was a refrigerator, did you? But you bought one because it sure is going to be a problem keeping your food out in the open!

Top Internet Entrepreneurs and Resellers know this principle very well, which also explains why exclusive product membership sites continue to thrive and grow.

Their selling point is **not in the product** but **the solutions and benefits** that come with the product.

Write with Personality

Now, we have come to an interesting part of writing your sales letter where people with strong personalities love to express themselves while others wish there was no such thing as personality.

I once heard the speaker at a Network Marketing seminar say, "*Talk with personality*". When you compose your sales letter, *write with personality*.

Don't write a stiff sales letter. Not only will it be boring, your prospects won't likely buy from you – unless they've got no personality, too.

Birds of a feather flock together. If you are fun and easy-going person, express yourself in such a manner in your sales letter.

Be friendly and approachable. If you are serious person, you write in a serious manner (but not *too* serious, it might just sell people away from your web page, and it is cheaper that way).

Remember that people of a kind attracts others of the same kind. This is a law written on stone. If you have to take a personality test on the Internet, please do. It will be worth your time!

And also, write casually. You may be in business but the key here is to write an *informal* letter. (Keyword: informal)

Address your prospect with *"Dear Friend"* and not *"Dear Sir"*.

Be personal and find how you can relate yourself to your prospects. If you are a break dance enthusiast, you can relate to your prospects your first six months of snapping every bone in your body before getting the power moves down.

You write with the understanding of the trouble and frustration your prospects are going through therefore you have the solution – you are going to teach your prospects how to break dance every step of the way with your how to videos!

The Power of Testimonials

Testimonials are powerful. They back what you have to say about your product in your sales letter. Good testimonials will encourage your prospects to purchase your product from you.

What to Have In Your Testimonials

- **Testimonials about YOUR product, not you**. Don't be fooled by the simplicity of this statement. Testimonials that say you are a great person whatsoever are NOT the type of testimonials your prospects are looking for, though such testimonials can build trust and your name. But your prospects are more interested in how your product can benefit them or solve their problems. They didn't read your sales letter to see you praising yourself.

- **Testimonials that mention results**. The more specific they are, the better. Interested prospects want to know what the results other customers have benefited from the usage of your product or service.

- **Quality / quantity**. If you can get top names in your niche or field to endorse your product, it will help your increase your sales. If you do not know any experts or top names who can help endorse your product, you can make up in the quantity of testimonials. The more testimonials you have, the more convincing your sales letter will be.

- **Customer essential details**. Include your customer's Full Name and City/State/Country after his or her testimonial. You can include your customer's web site URL or contact e-mail address where applicable (with permission). And if you can, get your customer's photo and paste it into your sales letter. Using photos can increase your credibility and shows how pleased your customers are when using your product.

How to Get Testimonials

- **Create a sample or mini version** of the main product you are selling. Give them to people close to you whom you think can benefit from your product. You can get their testimonials.

- **Get top names, influential people and experts to endorse your product**. So, look for top names and experts in your field and get their e-mail address. E-mail them and politely ask for their endorsement. Since they are only an e-mail away, why not? And if you

- You can **participate in active forums and newsgroups** where people of similar interest and mindset gather around and discuss on the same topic. This is a good place where you can meet people and get their testimonials simply by asking for their permission and give them a sample of your product. If your product is of genuine quality, you can count on them to send their honest testimonials in and spread the word for you.

Examples of How to Use Testimonials in Your Sales Letter

Case Study 1: Wizard Ads

http://www.wizardads.net/

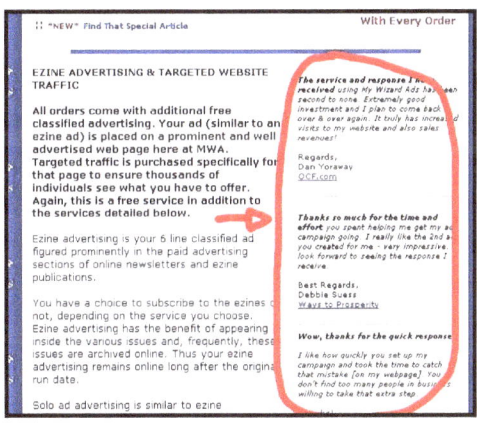

Note the testimonials by happy advertisers arranged neatly on your right. If you want to know more about the results of using this service, you can check with the testimonial writers who have left their web site URL under their names.

Case Study 2: Trafficology

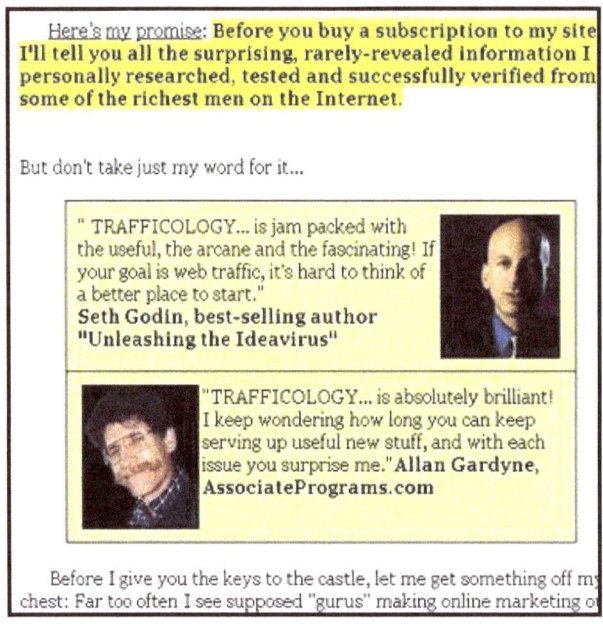

The top names are endorsing this service. Is there anymore doubt to using it if you need web site traffic?

Give a Guarantee

After telling your prospect all the wonderful things you product can do for him and proudly showcasing your precious testimonials, he is probably thinking, "That was good.

But should I be taking the risk to buy this product from you?"

And the answer is a resounding **NO**.

Purchasing anything online is risky. Don't blame your prospects for being scared. There are more idiots out there ready to rip and scam innocent people than you can count the stars in the night.

I don't know why they choose to be crooks when it is too easy to do business legally and in a harmonious manner but I guess I will never find out.

But you can find out how you can win your prospect's trust. Show your prospect that you are concerned and care for him.

And you can easily demonstrate this buy giving a money-back guarantee policy.

Usually, a money-back guarantee for digital product is <u>**90 days**</u>.

Here's an example of how your money-back guarantee policy may look like in your sales letter:

100% No-Nonsense Money Back Guarantee

Don't decide. **Just try it out!** Read it, apply the information within and get all set for your New Year's resolution... BIG TIME!

But if you feel that this is not what you are looking for, or that the information within are of no relevance or little help to your Internet Marketing success pursuit, you have a full 90 days to ask for a refund -- <u>no questions asked</u>. I am so confident that I can paste this guarantee policy here.

There is no way you can possibly lose.

This way, let your prospect know that you are shouldering all the risk for him.

Giving a money-back guarantee also demonstrates how confident you are in the quality of your product.

If for any reason your customer does not like your product or think it is not for him, he can promptly ask for a refund and delete the product from his PC. **Your prospect can't lose**.

A word on customer refunds: Being in business with your prospects can be risky for you as a vendor, too.

You will eventually learn that there are also idiots (no better word describes them) among your prospects that buy your product from your web page, and later ask for a refund (for the wrong reasons) and still keep your product!

Worst still, he copies your product to his contacts!

I am afraid that <u>nothing much</u> can be done. While you might be able to source for ways to protect your product as much as you can, it can be really effort and time-consuming to deal with these idiots.

Your time is best spent on improving or bringing in more revenue for your business.

Fortunately, there is only a minority of such people among the prospects in general. You can make up more in sales than the amount of refunds that they are almost negligible.

Welcome to the other world of Internet Entrepreneurship – something that most Internet Entrepreneurs won't talk about! :-)

Create Your Thank You Page

I may as well cover this while we're at it. Once you are done with your sales letter, it is time to create your Thank You Page.

Insert the link to your digital product for download in your Thank You Page. Include instructions for your customers to download the product.

Don't forget to write some kind words to thank your customers for doing business with you!

Download Problems?

While your delivery system is **automated** and your customer can download the product for himself, there is a small chance that the download may <u>not</u> be successful.

Maybe your customer got disconnected while he was downloading your product. Perhaps he accidentally exited your page.

Or you were careless to include the wrong link to your paid product! For whatever reasons he cannot download your product, leave your e-mail address on your Thank You Page for him to contact you.

And you'd better be sure to attend to it!

Give your word to your customer that you guarantee to respond to your customer's needs within <u>24-48 hours</u> when he has a problem.

Don't be a slacker at customer service – your customer is just *one click away* from asking for a refund.

How to Create a Back-End Sale in Your Thank You Page

Since we're covering this topic, we may as well take a short detour while I show you how you can earn extra from the same customer with no effort.

Selling a product only once is the quickest way to commit suicide financially. Novices do that, but not you. Now, let me show you what Top Internet Entrepreneurs do and be sure you follow them!

Did you know that your Thank You Page is a good place to **insert your advertisement or endorsement** for another product or service you either own or are an affiliate for?

This is what I call **back-end selling**.

Since your customer trusted you enough to buy your product from you for the first time, they will likely do it again.

And as long as the offered product or service at your Thank You Page has a lot to do with the product your customer has bought from you and he finds that it will benefit him as well, your chances of closing a sale is **high**.

This is how businesses operate – on **repeat customers**. And this applies to everywhere, online or offline.

You know you are smart when you place your **one-time offer** or **complimentary product or service** at your Thank You Page. You don't have to exert any marketing effort doing that, and it sure is rewarding for extra profits.

Setting Up Your Business

Not one model or approach is better than the other, as all 3 models can make money for you if done right. Check them all out below, and you can decide for yourself.

Model A

Setting Up Your Business Step-by-Step

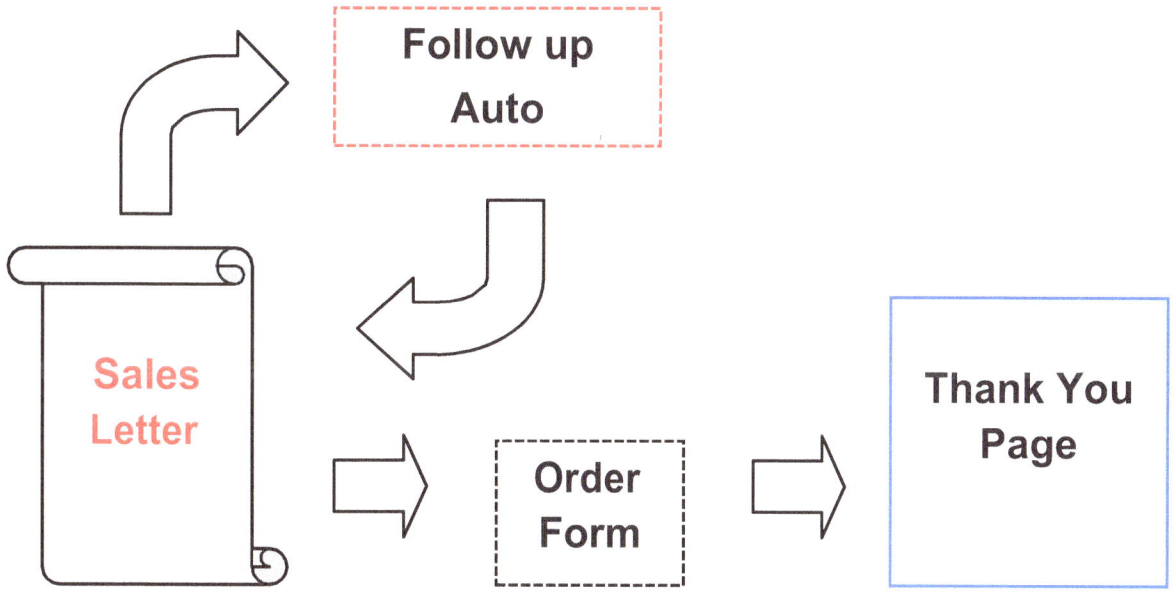

1. **Write your sales letter.**

    This has been discussed in detail in the previous chapter.

2. **Create your thank you page.**

This has been discussed in detail in the previous chapter.

3. **Write your series of follow up letters for your non-customers who opt into your mailing list.**

   As good as your sales letter conversion may be, a big number of your prospects will NOT buy your product or subscribe to your paid service at first contact.

   They might want to do a comparison between your product and other people's product, need more time to think about it, or leave your web page for whatever reason.

   And the truth is that we all can hardly remember where we were 10 web pages ago.

   So, the purpose of these letters stored within your auto responder is to automatically follow up with your non-buying prospects and continue persuading them to buy your product via email.

   A good follow up system will allow you to close sales even after your prospects have left your web page.

Write a series of follow up letters

Write a minimum of 4-8 follow up letters for your prospect. The objective of your follow up letters is to reveal more information not mentioned in your sales letter and later persuade your prospect to be your customer.

Your follow up letter need not be so long – around 400 to 750 words would be good enough.

In your follow up letter, you remind your prospect about your product, how it can benefit him, how it can save him money, time and effort, or how it can make him money.

1. **Sign up for an auto responder service.**

An auto responder is a computer program that automatically sends out pre-written email messages to subscribers within its data base.

You can determine the sequences and intervals of each of your messages, sparing you the time to manually follow up with your prospects.

You can sign up for a good auto responder service at [aWeber](#) for **$19.95 per month**.

You get to open unlimited auto responders and insert unlimited pre-written follow up messages. **aWeber** also handles the data entry of keeping your prospects details automatically.

You can opt to sign up for a **free** auto responder with unlimited storage of follow up messages at [Free Auto Bot](#).

Once done, store in your follow up letters and set their intervals.

The first letter will obviously be sent out instantly upon request by your prospect, followed by the second letter the next day, and third letter 3 days later, and the fourth another 3 days later, and so on.

2. **Install the pop up window script in your sales letter's HTML source code to appear the moment your prospect leaves the page.**

Install a pop up script in your sales letter to appear on your prospect's screen as soon as he exits your web page.

In the pop up page, you include a form where your prospect can fill in his name and email address, giving you permission to follow up with him later.

I know that some marketers have their pop up window appear the moment the prospect just arrived at the web page, but you won't want your prospect to know anything about the pop up in your sales letter YET as it will distract him or her from reading your sales letter thus decreasing the chance of closing the sale.

In the pop up page, you must convince your prospect to subscribe to your follow up series where you will disclose extra information and most importantly, convince your prospect to buy your product from you.

Recommended resource: I'm aware that many Internet users today have pop up killers installed in their browsers.

On top of that, a wrong approach by using pop ups can mean life or death for your business.

Having said that, I recommend you download Fly-In Ads Creator in your pop up creation effort. It's sold at $89.50 elsewhere, but you can download it [here](#) as part of your paid package.

3. **Get a domain name and web hosting.**

You need a web address for people to go to (e.g. [www.yourdomain.com](#)) and a web space to store your important documents such as your sales letter, thank you page and digital product(s).

You can register for a domain name under $10.00/year here:

[http://www.godaddy.com/](#)

[http://www.namecheap.com/](#)

You can register for affordable web hosting here:

[http://www.sitehost4u.com/](#)

[http://www.doteasy.com/](#)

Once you register both domain name and web hosting, upload all of your files into your web space using FTP (File Transfer Protocol) or file upload manager, if provided by the web host, in case you don't have or know how to use a FTP program.

4. Get a credit card payment processor.

You will need to use this to accept credit card payments, as it is the most often used method to pay online.

At this time of writing, I use 3 different payment processors.

Here are my recommended payment processors:

http://www.2checkout.com/

Requires $50.00 to start an account. Recommended for you if you are living in a country not supported by PayPal, as 2CheckOut.com is able to wire funds to almost every part of the world.

http://www.paypal.com/

This is by far the most popularly used payment processor online. Free to register, and the rates are already at its lowest.

Insert the pay button into the bottom of your sales letter and route to your Thank You page URL where your customer can get the product are the purchase.

Have this done, and upload your sales letter into your web host. Double check everything and perhaps make a test transaction to see if your download and system are working. You are ready to go!

Model B

Setting Up Your Business Step-by-Step

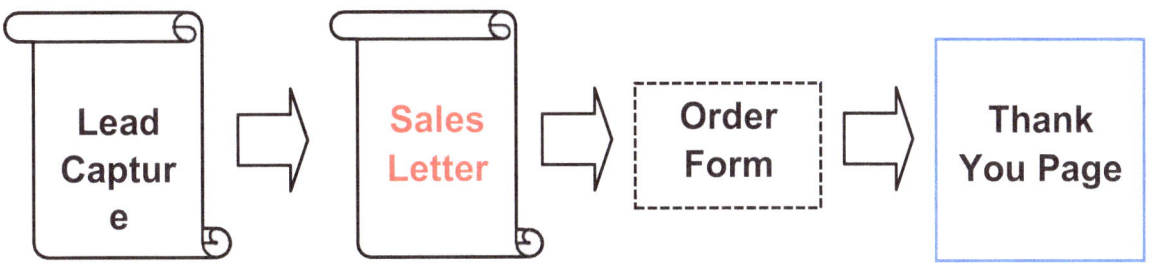

This model is slightly different from the former, where you collect your subscriber's lead first and later bring him to your sales letter.

Write your lead capture page.

This page is somewhat a preview to what you are going to offer to your prospect.

On this page, you can give:

- A free report (to be send to your prospect's email address),

- A trial version of your product,

- A teaser to your product, and/or

- An incentive for your prospect to subscribe to your mailing list for future mailing list and useful information (don't forget to give them offers, too!)

For examples, see [Megapreneur Millions](#) and [List Builder Pro](#). After having opted into your mailing list, redirect your prospects to your sales letter.

1. **Write your follow up series.**

Depending on what you are offering in your Lead Capture Page, write your follow up series to be automatically sent out to your prospects.

If you are sending out a series of letters on tips, write 4 to 8 letters to be sent on auto-pilot via auto responder.

If you are giving a free report or trial product, include the link to your product in the first email.

If you are going to alert your prospects on future offers you may have, such as a promoting a product or service you are affiliated with, you will do well to get your prospects to confirm their participation in your mailing list.

- **Get an auto responder.**

    This step has been discussed in detail in Model A.

- **Write your sales letter.**

    This step has been discussed in detail in the previous chapter.

- **Create your thank you page.**

    This step has been discussed in detail in the previous chapter.

- **Get domain name and web hosting.**

    This step has been discussed in detail in Model A. Once you get your domain name and web hosting, upload all of your files via FTP or file upload manager.

- **Get a credit card payment processor.**

This step has been discussed in detail in Model A.

Model C

Setting Up Your Business Step-by-Step

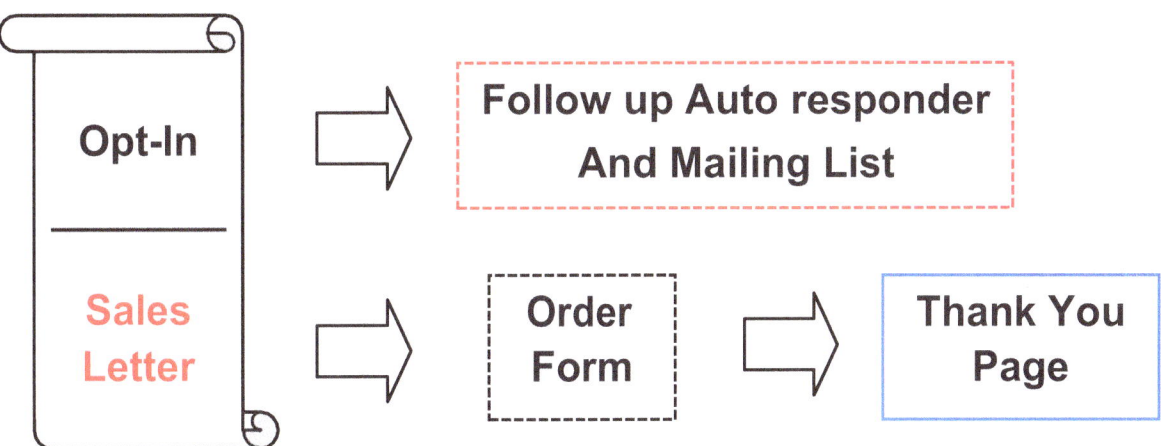

This is probably the trickiest model of all 3 models, and it will depend heavily on how well you write your sales letter.

1. **Write your sales letter.**

The first half of your sales letter is aimed at squeezing for your subscriber's email address. Thus the first part of the letter is to persuade your subscriber to into your mailing list.

You can:

- Give a free report or trial version of your product, and/or
- Offer some valuable information for free,

This would mean including the "opt in" form on the letter itself.

Tip: Remember to redirect your prospect back to the same letter to continue reading the other part of the letter.

The other half of the letter is obviously aimed at selling your product to your prospect, where everything in "writing a letter that sells" takes off from here.

The rest of these steps are self explanatory, and are similar to the steps highlighted in Models A and B earlier.

2. Write your follow up letters.

3. Sign up for an auto responder.

4. Create your thank you page.

6. Get domain name and web hosting.

7. Get a credit card payment processor.

Pros

Model A

- You get to convert prospects into customers upfront.
- You can later follow up with non-buyers and still get a chance at converting them into your customer or affiliate.

Model B

- You get narrow down the focus of your sales letter prospecting.

- You get to build your mailing list faster compared to Models A and C, since the first thing required of your prospect before reading your sales letter is to opt into your mailing list.

- You can later follow up with your prospects on other offers if they are not going to buy your product as you already have their permission to opt into your mailing list.

Model C

- You get to have your prospect opt into your mailing list and still buy your product on the same visit.

- You can later follow up with your prospects on other offers if they are not going to buy your product as you already have their permission to opt into your mailing list.

Cons

Model A

- You cannot build your mailing list as fast as Model B, given the same amount of traffic.

- If you are using a regular pop up window, it may be blocked by several prospects whose browsers have "banner killer" functions set on.

Model B

- With your Lead Capture Page, you will be eliminating and narrowing your search a lot, and if not done right, the number of prospects who visit your sales letter will be much less than expected.

Model C

- Doing this model involves good copywriting skills, since the focus of the letter itself is divided into two.

In the Next Manual...

You're not really done yet, even after setting up your business. We still have **one last aspect** on your paperless E-Book publishing success that needs catching up. See you in the last series!

Recommended Resources

Edmund Loh's 8 Profit-Pulling PLR Strategies That Really Work! – unlock the secrets to making money with Private Label Rights using 8 totally unique, killer strategies!

19 Internet Business Models – eliminate guesswork and discover what makes the world go round for Internet Entrepreneurs and copy their success business systems for your own in a flash – low cost, high profit!

All-in-One E-Commerce Solutions

SOLOBIS – all-in-one solution comes with unlimited web hosting, domain name, unlimited auto responders, broadcast feature, custom web builder, file manager, link cloakers, JV manager, 500+ beautiful web templates, online support team, and many more. No HTML and programming knowledge required.

Recommended Payment Processors

2CheckOut.com – start accepting credit card payments from customers from several parts of the world!

Module 3: Online Marketing Explained

Dear Valued Reader,

It's already time. Your business is all set up and it's time to do one last thing – **marketing**.

Your business should be marketed to none other than your target prospects. Some call this "driving traffic" but in a real sense, it would be more accurate if you call it "driving <u>targeted</u> traffic".

It's common sense marketing, anyway.

There are real people on the other side of the phone line, and they have to have the criteria of a targeted prospect in order to increase the chance of you making the sale.

In a nutshell, the criteria of a <u>targeted</u> prospect are:

- Already looking for your product (demand), and
- Have money to spend!

It is that simple. This is why you won't find me endorsing guaranteed traffic. While the thought of having 1 million visitors over at your web site for only $29.99 is amusing, it's insulting your intelligence when you follow the above criteria of a targeted prospect.

We're talking about having 1 million **real** people, prospecting to buy YOUR product.

For example, if you are selling a book aimed at dog owners, what are the chances that the 1 million visitors are all dog owners?

Some of them could be cat owners, some wrestle with crocodiles, and the rest probably don't even own a pet!

This is another good reason **NOT** to purchase bulk email addresses from so-called companies.

Ever wonder how you get emails about Viagra, as if everyone thinks you are looking for one?

Therefore, if you are selling a book for dog owners and using this solicited marketing tactic, everyone else will be wondering why you're thinking they have a dog in the first place.

You will also discover why I am not keen to recommend Search Engine Optimization to you as a primary method of marketing your Info Product business, though I will be covering some grounds on it shortly.

With some of several questionable marketing methods axed out from this manual, you will come to conclude that **<u>not every marketing method is for every kind of Internet Business</u>**.

As in the case of your own paperless E-Book publishing, you will discover what **really works** for this particular business.

For anything less than great won't settle within the coming pages.

Get gamed for serious profits – this is the last round!

To Your Paperless E-Book Publishing Success!

The Truth about SEO

Adding your web site to the major Search Engines' list is one of the first steps you should take towards marketing your business.

However, if you would ask me, I do not find it wise to fully rely on getting visitors through the Search Engines.

This is probably a ground where SEO experts wouldn't agree with me. But consider the following scenario:

With every Internet Marketer of any niche being told, taught and motivated to score for a number one listing in major Search Engines, you can bet it's a free-for-all battle between marketers to have their web site listed as number one for a ==hot== keyword.

While getting your site listed in the first 3 pages of search results in major Search Engines can be considered a success, since visitors in general are patient enough to view the first 3 pages of the search results, it probably won't be worth the fight.

I haven't factor in that Search Engine rules and algorithms do change from time to time, resulting in your listing dropping from no. 1 to rock-bottom in manner of days or weeks.

Yes, some people do come over and tell me, "My site is number one in the listing for [insert keyword here]." To them I often say this, "So did mine!"

By this, I also want to demonstrate to you that Search Engine Optimization or SEO in short, is about **capitalizing on keywords that people search for in masses.**

Putting it in other words, you need to capitalize on niche keywords where people are willing to spend money on. Obviously, your name is not a niche.

No one are going online specifically to look for me, and are not willing to spend money just for the sake of fulfilling the "whatever your name is" demand, unless you are a celebrity.

While you can count on Search Engine traffic, you will be cheating yourself of better, more sophisticated marketing methods that can help you reach to more prospects.

Submitting Your Site to Search Engines

We will still have this ground covered before moving on to other marketing methods that work best for your Info Product Empire.

The list below gives you direct links to the submission pages:

- **Yahoo.com** (www.yahoo.com)

1. Go to directory under which you want to submit a site.

2. Click the "**Suggest a Site**" link.

Non-business categories are free to submit to, but it can take awhile to get listed. Business categories will cost you $299 a year. (Personal recommendation: keep your money!)

- **Open Directory Project (dmoz)**

1. Go to http://www.dmoz.org.

2. Browse to the directory where you think your site belongs.

3. Click the "**Add Url**" link at the top of the page.

This is a key directory to get into as a great deal of Search Engines use their database to show results.

- **Google**

Go to: http://www.google.com/addurl.html

They will generally find your site to index for their database, even if you don't manually submit it. They use the dmoz results as part of their database.

Usually, submitting to these Search Engines would do.

This is because while there are thousands more of Search Engines out there (and comes the service that claims they'll submit your site to thousands of Search Engines), the truth is that majority of those Search Engines are nowhere near as heavily trafficked as Google and Yahoo!

Preparing Your Promotion Materials

You're going to need to prepare your marketing materials first-hand before starting any one or more of the marketing methods in the coming pages, whether it is for your own use or your affiliate's convenience in helping you market your business.

Endorsement Letter

If you own a mailing list, you will need to send a letter to your subscribers, telling them about your latest product.

Your affiliates with mailing lists will appreciate using your endorsement letter as well (where they can use, rewrite, or edit a little), because you will be saving them time and effort from having to write their own from scratch.

Your letter need not be long – 200 to 500 words would do. Your letter is basically a teaser on your product and the purpose is to get the subscriber to click on the link to go to your sales letter.

Call it pre-selling if you want to, but you need to spark up your prospect's interest first to venture on into your sales page.

Here is an example of an endorsement letter:

Subject: {firstname}, Awesome Private Label Rights Offer

Hi {firstname},

You and I know that one of the sure fire ways to succeed online is to own your own product. No, I'm not talking about Resell Rights, but about having at least one product with YOUR NAME on it.

Having your own products gives you full control, flexibility and ownership over your product and business. And to top that up, selling Information Products is the *best* way to make your money online.

But then, it is often "easier said than done".

The good news, though, is that John Doe has put together a collection of quality, products with editable Private Label Rights, with each of them catering to hot, in-demand markets.

That means you can edit the contents, change the title, put your own affiliate links in, and even put your name on it as the author on these products! Imagine the amount of time, effort and money you can save from having to create your own Info Products, doing market research, hiring professional services, and much, much more!

I got my hands onto Edmund's package and I found out that calling it a fascinating deal is truly an understatement, because it was not a couple of "Fear Factor" dishes he offered, but just a darn, good bargain!

I could go on to tell you what a good offer it is, but you will do well to check out the full details below with your own bare eyes:

---

http://www.privatelabelrightsgold.com/ (Note to JV partner: Replace the link above with your JV link and remove this paragraph)

Warm Regards,

{Insert Your Name Here}

P.S. You can check out the full details in the link above, to learn why this is a stunning Private Label Rights offer.

Solo Ads

Solo ads are usually short ads that resemble those you often find in the newspaper's classified ads section.

If you and/or your affiliate run your own online newsletters with ad spaces, you and/or your affiliate can insert solo ads for your subscribers to view.

Your solo ad can be like the following:

===

Finally! Discover How You Can Easily Skip the Product

Creation Process and Acquire a Collection of Products You

Which Can Put Your Name as the Author, Change Their Titles,

Edit Their Contents, Put In Your Affiliate Links, and More!

http://www.privatelabelrightsgold.com/

If your affiliate often invests in E-zine advertising, he will most likely use your solo ad to submit to E-zines he or she paid advertising for.

Banners

Banners can come in the form of text or image.

A banner text can be as simple as a one-liner, such as one used by my affiliate below:

SureFireWealth.com

http://www.surefirewealth.com/

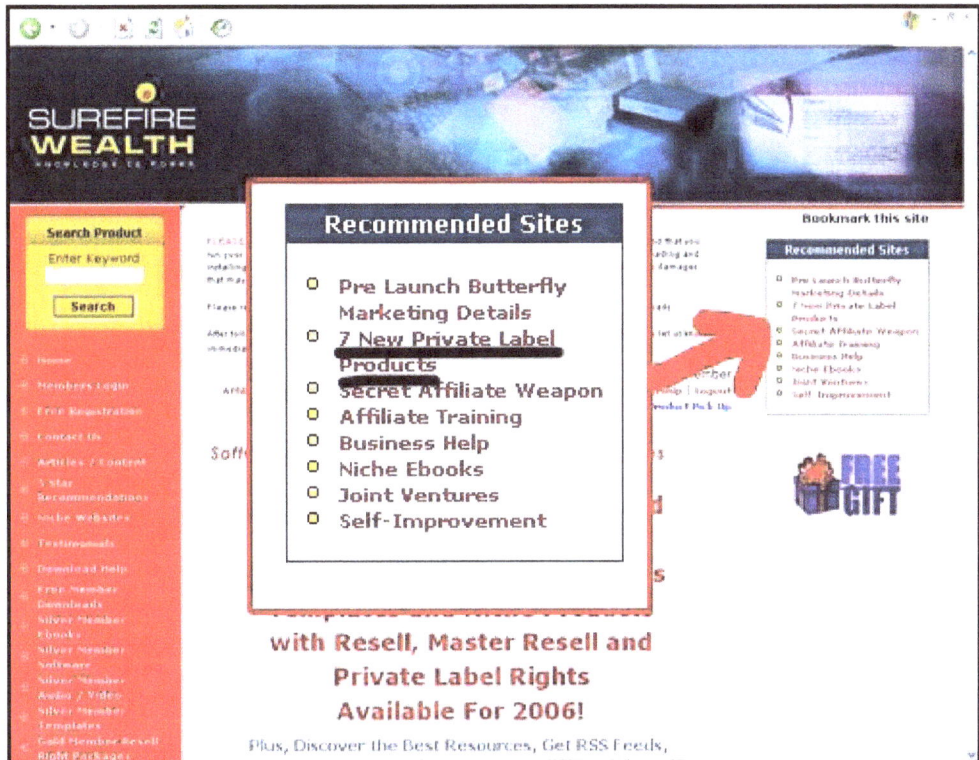

Banners can also come in image form. Here's an example of an image banner:

http://www.privatelabelrightsgold.com/jv/images/banner_468x60.gif

468x60 pixels

Signature File

This is one often used when you send/reply emails or post at forums. My own signature (sig) file is written:

John Doe

Own 7 *Hot* Products with Private Label Rights!

http://www.privatelabelrightsgold.com/

Endorsing to Your Mailing List

This is definitely the **fastest** way to get the word out – endorsing your product to your mailing list.

Once you get your endorsement letter written out, you just need to paste it into your auto responder broadcast feature and send it out to your subscribers.

That can be true… <u>only if you have one</u>!

If you haven't got a mailing list, don't sweat just yet. As taught in Component #2 of this series, you will increase both your opt-in subscribers AND sales as long as you drive in targeted prospects (or traffic if you would prefer to call it) with effort, regardless of whichever one of the 3 business models you choose to design after.

The result would be that **you will build your own mailing list alongside with making sales of your product**.

And when you come up with a second Info Product, you can approach the list of subscribers you have built from your first product!

Now, you know why it's worth mentioning this to you.

Just a reminder, though, that in your Lead Capture Page or "Thank you for subscribing" email, do let your subscriber know that you will give him or her special offers once in a while, so they won't get alarmed the next time you endorse a new Info Product you've created

Leverage on Affiliate Marketing

Leveraging one's marketing efforts on affiliates has been the way to go for many Info Product business owners, and will be in the years to come.

As explained earlier in Component #2 of the Info Product Empire series, an affiliate acts very similar to a referrer, and gets paid for every successful referral sale.

You don't mind giving up anywhere from **40% to 75%** of your product sale to your affiliate because:

- Your profit margin is about 100%,

- There is no cost incurred in delivering the digital Info Product, and

- Your affiliate has freed you a lot from your marketing efforts!

After all, an army of affiliates working at the same time to promote your business will definitely make **more money** than if you would've worked on your own, even though you get to keep the entire profits.

Recommended Resources For Starting Your Own Affiliate Program

- <http://paydotcom.com/>

    Opening an account with PayDotCom.com is free. You need to have [PayPal](#) and/or [StormPay](#) to receive payments from customers and send commissions to your affiliates. The premier account enables you to add unlimited product lines for sale for a one-off $29.00. If you are selling only one product, the free account is sufficient.

- <http://www.clickbank.com/>

    While this requires a first-time payment of $50.00, ClickBank is one of the earliest and most established credit card payment processor and affiliate program in the Internet marketplace, displaying a wide variety of products in its marketplace catalog.

Recruiting Affiliates

1. Submitting your affiliate program to affiliate program directories. Some heavily-trafficked affiliate program directories include:

    <http://www.associateprograms.com/>

http://www.refer-it.com/

http://www.linkshare.com/

http://www.lifetimecommissions.com/

http://www.affiliatesdirectory.com/

Tip: If you want to save your time submitting to major affiliate directories, you can do it once by submitting your affiliate programs here for a one-time fee of $59.00.

http://www.affiliatefirst.com/submit

2. Convert some of your prospects into affiliates via a small link at the bottom of your sales letter. Including a small link that reads "Become an Affiliate" at the bottom of your sales letter can convert some of your non-buyers into affiliates. That's better than letting them go loose, right?

3. You can convert some of your prospects into affiliates via your mailing list's auto responder.

    After a certain number of days and a series of follow up mails, you can give a one-last-time offer by having your prospect join your affiliate army and help sell your product for a decent commission. Remember to include your affiliate program sign up link!

4. You can have your customers become your affiliates, too, by offering a sign up link to your affiliate program in your Thank You page, the page

where your customer will go to download the product. You can pitch in that they can cover back their investment by telling others about your product! Oh, and <u>without</u> spamming, of course!

Giving Your Affiliates What They Need

Regardless of how and which way you run your affiliate program, be sure to give your affiliates all the marketing materials they will need to spread the word out.

Remember me asking you to write out your endorsement letters, banners and solo ads earlier?

They will come in just as handy for this purpose.

The logic behind this is that you want to make sure your affiliates have less chores (and excuses) possible as their efforts should **focus solely on marketing and nothing else.**

One thing you must note though, that not every affiliate is equal or just as motivated as the other.

As a matter of fact, only a small percentage, as in 1% to 5%, of the affiliates will be the ones producing results for your affiliate sales.

Thus it is up to you to comb the Internet marketplace in search for super affiliates who have huge mailing lists and incredible marketing power.

One last thing to note is that every savvy affiliate often looks into the aspects of your affiliate program:

- Your product and quality,
- Your product's demand,
- The commission incentives,
- How well your sales letter is written.

Having said that, you will need to be top-notch in all of the above-mentioned areas in order to recruit savvy affiliates with great marketing power because even a super affiliate can match the marketing power of 100, maybe 1,000 average affiliates.

Ad Swaps

This is often a very under-used technique, but it is very effective for a **no-brainer** marketing method. It's free anyway, thus your ROI can be infinite! :-)

I personally call it "using subscribers to make subscribers", but an ad swap works this way: you trade showing advertisements with other mailing list owners.

Assuming you and another mailing list owner each has 1,000 subscribers; you barter with him by endorsing his ad to your mailing list. In exchange, he also endorses YOUR ad to his mailing list.

And if the mailing list owner or newsletter publisher has 2,000 subscribers, for example, he just need to endorse your ad once while you endorse his twice to make up for the numbers.

It makes sense anyway. After all, you are likely to swap ads with a direct competitor so both you and him can compliment each other as the natures of your subscribers are similar.

This method works **best** if:

- You already have a list of subscribers (at least 800 to 1,000), and

- You are using Model B, as highlighted in Module #2 of this unique series.

Now, you want your ad to focus on **collecting subscriber leads first**. You want to collect and cultivate your relationship with your prospects that just came from another mailing list.

It would be unwise to directly promote your sales letter page in your ad as you've got only ONE shot at your prospects to make a sale. Some may buy, the rest won't.

And when the rest of your prospects leave your page, they probably won't come back again as the rest of the web pages are screaming for their attention.

As all 3 models have a way to collect subscriber leads, Model B works best for this ad swap method as the first thing required of the prospect is to opt into your mailing list.

You can automatically follow up with him or her later even after he leaves your page. Secondly, you may offer him something else if your primary product doesn't appeal to him.

In a real sense, **don't just let anyone get away from your site!**

Where to Look for E-zine Publishers to Swap Ads With

>http://www.directoryofE-zines.com/

>http://www.warriorforum.com/forum (see JV section)

>http://www.jvnotifypro.com/

Low Cost Advertising that Works

Paid E-zine Advertising

E-zine advertising is very affordable advertising method that can enable you to reach **hundreds of thousands** of prospects with as low as <u>**under $50.00**</u>. And in some E-zine advertising offers, your investment can be as low as under $10.00.

Your investment returns can be virtually high – with a few ifs and buts, of course.

In a nutshell, you are buying advertising space in other people's E-zines. In offline terms, it is as if you are buying classified ad space in the local papers.

When the E-zine publisher sends out his or her next issue out to his or her subscribers, your ad will be published together and get read by thousands of subscribers.

The critical success factors in paid E-zine advertising are:

- ✓ **How targeted the subscribers are.**

- ✓ **How responsive the subscribers are.**

- ✓ **How many subscribers are there?** The more subscribers you can reach to, the better.

- ✓ **How compellingly written your ad copy is.** If you are not good ad writing, investing a few extra dollars on decent ad writing and your investment will pay off.

Here are also some important questions you should ask potential E-zine publishers whom you consider buying advertising space from:

- o What is the nature of the E-zine?

- o What kind of prospects subscribe to your E-zine?

- o How responsive are the prospects?

- o How many subscribers are there in your E-zine?

Recommended E-zine Advertising Resources

Here is some of the paid E-zine advertising I have used and trusted. Therefore, I can proudly recommend them to you.

http://www.mywizardads.com/

http://www.E-zines-r-us.com/

http://www.admistress.com/

Affiliate Program Submission

If you want to save your time submitting to major affiliate directories, you can do it once by submitting your affiliate programs here for a one-time fee of $59.00.

http://www.affiliatefirst.com/submit

Pay-Per-Click (PPC)

PPC advertising refers to any type of advertising where you pay for every click-through.

PPC advertisers pay webmasters to put their advertisements on their website.

The advertisers are then charged on a "per click" basis when a visitor clicks on their ads on those sites.

The webmaster gets paid when some one clicks on the ads on their website.

Important! Make sure your sales page **converts well** because once your prospects have clicked through to see your web page, it is either a make or break in the sale.

If not, at least strive to collect their email addresses for follow ups (which will not be a problem as long as you follow any one of the 3 business models described in the last component of the series).

Since the higher you pay per bid, the higher your ad ranking will be, here is a school of thought you should subscribe to: Never bid on a general keyword!

For instance, you may be selling a product that caters to the dating market.

Obviously, keywords such as "dating" and "relationship" are too general.

Dating isn't ALL about women, since there are also men to make the love circle complete and not to mention the bi-sexual (oops! :-X).

It is crucial, really. Instead, you should be more specific on your keywords related to your product or service.

Bid your keywords wisely and you will get the kind of prospects you are looking for.

Again, using the same example above, if you are bidding on keywords such as "dating service", "dating advice", "dating tips", etc. you can almost bet that the only kind of person looking and using phrases and keywords like these is a serious lover in the making. :-)

Recommended PPC Search Engines

http://www.overture.com/

http://www.search123.com/

http://www.kanoodle.com/

http://www.goclick.com/

Buy Subscribers

You can buy subscribers from list brokers for as low as 10 cents a name.

This way, you can quickly build your mailing list and convert a percentage of them into your customers.

Recommended Subscriber List Brokers

http://ww.hiplists.com/

http://www.listpartners.com/

http://www.listbuilderpro.com/

http://www.rankyou.com/

The Closing

Hi, it's me again and we're drawing close to an end of the paperless E-Book publishing series.

Remember, the <u>ultimate</u> purposes of your web site are none other than to:

- ✓ Sell your product, and
- ✓ Build your mailing list!

It is that simple.

It is true that in business, a proven system that works is the most important, with which if you know how to build one, you can then spawn countless products, ideas and concepts.

Now, armed with all the knowledge and information you need to know to build your first Info Product out of thin air (with what you already have to cash from your most important asset, your mind!), your next Internet Marketing success awaits your first step to taking action! :-)

To Your Paperless E-Book Publishing Success!

Recommended Resources

[Edmund Loh's 8 Profit-Pulling PLR Strategies That Really Work!](#) – unlock the secrets to making money with Private Label Rights using 8 totally unique, killer strategies!

[19 Internet Business Models](#) – eliminate guesswork and discover what makes the world go round for Internet Entrepreneurs and copy their success business systems for your own in a flash – low cost, high profit!

All-in-One E-Commerce Solutions

[SOLOBIS](#) – all-in-one solution comes with unlimited web hosting, domain name, unlimited auto responders, broadcast feature, custom web builder, file manager, link cloakers, JV manager, 500+ beautiful web templates, online support team, and many more. No HTML and programming knowledge required.

Recommended Payment Processors

2CheckOut.com – start accepting credit card payments from customers from several parts of the world!

www.ingramcontent.com/pod-product-compliance
Lightning Source LLC
Chambersburg PA
CBHW060422220526
45465CB00008B/2977